New Orleans
The First 300 Years

Edited by Errol Laborde and Peggy Scott Laborde
Foreword by Lawrence N. Powell

PELICAN PUBLISHING COMPANY
GRETNA 2018

First printing, August 2017
Second printing, January 2018

The word "Pelican" and the depiction of a pelican are trademarks of Pelican Publishing Company, Inc., and are registered in the U.S. Patent and Trademark Office.

Library of Congress Cataloging-in-Publication Data

Names: Laborde, Errol, 1947- editor. | Peggy Scott Laborde, editor.
Title: New Orleans : the first 300 years / Errol Laborde and Peggy
    Scott Laborde, editors.
Description: Gretna : Pelican Publishing Company, 2017. | Includes index.
Identifiers: LCCN 2017013772| ISBN 9781455621606 (hardcover : alk.
    paper) |
    ISBN 9781455621613 (e-book)
Subjects: LCSH: New Orleans (La.)—History.
Classification: LCC F379.N557 N49 2017 | DDC 976.3/35—dc23 LC record
    available at https://lccn.loc.gov/2017013772

New Orleans/Law intersection photograph on front jacket by Sally Asher

Printed in the United States of America
Published by Pelican Publishing Company, Inc.
1000 Burmaster Street, Gretna, Louisiana 70053
www.pelicanpub.com

Contents

How History Saved New Orleans

Lawrence N. Powell

Not long after the levees failed, when New Orleanians were still mucking out their homes and challenging their adjusters' drive-by appraisals, an existential angst took hold that, maybe, New Orleans' days were numbered. The streets were cratered worse than Kabul's. An ancient infrastructure—gas and water mains, sewerage lines and drainage conduits, buried under eons of compacted mud—had been crushed beneath the weight of millions of tons of standing water. There was the standoff between residents and local businesses over who should rebuild first. That's when cheap shots rained down from some national politicians and divines, suggesting our semi-ruined city could stand a good flattening. "It looks like a lot of that place could be bulldozed," then-Speaker of the US House of Representatives Dennis Hastert told an Illinois newspaper.

Defeatism has never found lasting favor with a people who like to view death as a chance for putting the "fun" in "funeral." The stiff upper lip stems from a resilience forged by centuries of storms, floods, and scourges. New Orleans is an astonishingly rooted community. There are families here, black and white, who trace their ancestry back three, four, even eight generations. After Katrina, people returned to New Orleans for a galaxy of reasons. They had the resources to do so. They missed the red beans and the R&B or the way folks banter at the checkout counter. But an untold number returned, as Lolis Eric Elie has said, "because our grandfather built this house." So there was no question New Orleanians would hunker down to prove the scoffers wrong. This quirky town was worth saving, even if it meant stripping down to the studs and starting over. Did New Orleans have a future? The answer was a resounding yes.

Yet, perhaps because I'm a professional historian, I can't help but feel this stubborn faith in the city's future, so critical to the post-Katrina recovery, was also linked to its history. New Orleans is a town where identity inheres in a sense of place over time. There's the attitude: We're somebody. We come from somewhere. Look at our history, which, by the way, is impossible to escape. You stumble on it every time you step over a sidewalk buckled by the roots of ancient live oaks. It's in the ambience of a place that can't decide whether it's a city or a sound stage.

But there is a big problem. In the Big Easy, separating fact from fiction is never easy. Mythmakers have tenanted New Orleans' past with a surfeit of ghosts and vampires, never mind enough privateers to ransack a treasure fleet. But, honestly, the romance has nothing on the real history. And to appreciate the one, you have to understand the other; you have to squint into the present through the lens of bygone days. It is what historians mean by "perspective."

§

Although New Orleans has had a 300-year run, not every century has received equal billing. In historical compilations, the third act has received the shortest shrift, which is unfortunate. The twentieth century was every bit as consequential as the centuries preceding it. Traditional jazz, for example, that wind ensemble of joyous polyphony, flowered at that century's dawning; R&B and rock 'n' roll blossomed in its middle years. Jim Crow segregation and disfranchisement rose and fell during the same span of time. Furthermore, it was slightly more than a hundred years ago when the back swamp was drained—with home-grown technology that Holland borrowed to dry up the Zuiderzee—enabling suburban expansion toward the lake. Then there was the mini-manufacturing boom (the only one in the city's long history) that occurred during World War II, followed a quarter century later by the oil and gas industry's glass-tower transformation of Poydras Street. Tourism became an organized behemoth after 1945, just in time for the modern preservation movement to save the French Quarter from bulldozing, defilement, and demolition by neglect. In the 1920s, a Dixie Bohemia of famous and not-so-famous novelists and artists expatriated to the nostalgic decay of the French Quarter—by then a Little Palermo—inaugurating a tradition of literary slumming that has scarcely abated. As for our culinary culture, not until the twentieth century did it mature into a full-throated tradition. Then there are New Orleans' outsize politics and those notorious machine-gun standoffs between Huey Long and the New Orleans machine.

That being said, not all epochs are equal. Some possess special valence. The messy colonial era is one, for instance, starting with Bienville's fateful decision in 1718 to plant an urban grid in a flood-prone fever swamp. Although a few early boosters were over the moon about the new town's foreordained greatness, the truth is, that punishing location pretty much doomed New Orleans to economic insignificance until the eve of the American takeover. Paris virtually abandoned the Creole capital when it became a money pit. New Orleanians from across the social spectrum embraced smuggling as a survival virtue. And when the plantation system collapsed into frontier lassitude, idled slaves were told to hunt and fish and raise vegetables to feed themselves as well as town and country folk alike, earning small savings along the way. Hustling entered New Orleans' bloodstream during these years. So did an appreciation for the values that made survival worthwhile. To push back against the grime and peril of daily existence, the town's underclass, black and white, crowded into roistering cabarets in the back of town while the elite partied as if there was no tomorrow (which was often the case because of high mortality rates), their womenfolk cradling ball gowns as they splashed through the mud to attend yet one more soirée.

For over thirty years, New Orleans was a Spanish colony. France ceded Louisiana to Madrid in 1763 as a sort of consolation prize for territorial losses incurred during the Seven Years' War. Within Spain's overseas commercial empire, Louisiana was a poor fit. That didn't deter Spain from sinking money into New Orleans. Most of the colonial-era structures extant in the Vieux Carré were erected by Spanish treasure following devastating fires in 1788 and 1794. Another Latin American institution also dates back to the days of the dons: New Orleans' distinctive community of *gens de couleur libres,* free people of color. Although this Afro-Creole caste had started forming during the French period, it wasn't until Spanish governors established a free black militia and sanctioned a regime of slave self-purchase that it achieved a kind of critical mass. This was when the hustling sector of the slave community began drawing down their cumulative savings to buy themselves—and their families—out of slavery.

By the time of the Louisiana Purchase, New Orleans, a town scarcely larger than 8,000 permanent residents, had morphed into an established culture not easily swept aside. The old inhabitants were attached to their Roman law traditions, their language, their sensual pleasures. Americans came to conquer, which they eventually did, but at a cultural price. No less than the German, Irish, and Italians who poured into New Orleans throughout the nineteenth century, they too had to assimilate to an alternative Afro-European society. It is no exaggeration to say that tone and spirit of contemporary New Orleans still show the stretch marks of that early encounter between the city's Latin past and Anglo-American future.

§

The history of any place—town, city, state—seesaws between change and continuity. It can be gradual and then sudden or not change at all. But if there is one epoch where change charged ahead and the city was transformed beyond recognition from what had come before, it was New Orleans' antebellum heyday. The Crescent City came of age during these years—roughly 1815 to 1860—and along with it, so did American capitalism, the explosive growth of one tightly coupled with the quicksilver development of the other. The change happened with almost hallucinatory speed. At the time of the American takeover, New Orleans was little more than a backwater of empire. Six decades later, following a hothouse period of unrivaled growth, she had vaulted into the front rank of American cities. Powering the demographic surge was New Orleans' sudden emergence as the commercial emporium of the Mississippi Valley, the greatest free trade zone the world had seen up till then. The valley was filling fast with small farmers and small towns. Until the 1830s, they were landlocked behind the Appalachian mountain chain. This was an age when trade followed the rivers, before canals connected the East with the Great Lakes and railroad trunk lines united New York and Chicago. Those natural waterways mainly flowed south, usually into the Mississippi River, the greatest artery of commerce of them all. And perched near the mouth was New Orleans, her wharves literally straddling the strategic narrows of commerce. Steamboats heralded this new world aborning. The first one arrived in January 1812, steaming through the angry waters of the New Madrid earthquake. By 1860, over 3,500 steamboats were arriving yearly, flooding levees already heaped with pork, grain, and whiskey with additional acres of cotton and sugar. *DeBow's Review*, New Orleans' and the South's leading business journal, barely exaggerated when it declared: "No city of the world has ever advanced as a mart of commerce with such gigantic and rapid strides as New Orleans."

But market revolutions aren't the products of spontaneous generation. It takes a very, very large village to build them out. In New Orleans, it was a hard-charging merchant class who wielded the biggest hammer. Most were outsiders, either from the Ohio Valley and the Upper South or, more likely, from the Atlantic seaboard—New York and Boston, for example, as well as Philadelphia and Baltimore. Not a few came from London and Paris, even Tampico, Mexico. Joining them were a cadre of ambitious and remarkably talented lawyers, a few from revolutionary-wracked France and Saint-Domingue but the vast generality from the same common law states as their commercial associates. New Orleans was the new Calcutta for getting rich quick and returning home to live it up. All that was necessary was to throw up one or two warehouses and organize a chaotic marketplace. It was these business pioneers who populated today's CBD with commission houses and factorage firms. They founded marine insurance companies and built cotton presses. They launched vast infrastructural projects, subdividing one plantation after another to house a booming population now bursting at the city's seams. And, because antebellum America lacked a uniform currency and depended upon banks to create money, the rising establishment incorporated an array of specialized banks to finance the city's burgeoning commerce and redirect into the Mississippi Valley the torrents of capital pouring into New Orleans from England, Europe, and New York—capital that literally built the internal commerce of the American continent. Initially, western produce and Louisiana sugar concentrated New Orleans' commercial attention; by 1830, it was cotton and slaves (on whom, more shortly) that commanded her energies. And as that transition took place, the Crescent City's money market emerged as one of the most vital banking centers in the country, second only to New York. Indeed, in the way of sheer volume, New Orleans' banking institutions probably surpassed Gotham in the amount of business paper that it discounted. Meanwhile, the newly established Louisiana Bar (there wasn't one to speak of prior to the Purchase), together with the post-Purchase court system, carried out the mundane but profitable work of improvising commercial rules—rules regarding such arcane matters as partnerships, marine insurance, and negotiable instruments—essential to the smooth functioning of a dynamic market. We like to think of New Orleans as a world-class enjoyment culture. The truth is, there was a time when it was also an epicenter of capitalist development.

Then there were the tides of immigration that lapped at New Orleans shores during her glamour decades. The largest tide deposited waves of Irish and Germans on the levee, along with a continuing stream of French transplants and even newcomers from southern Europe, the Balkans, and points farther east. The years 1835 to 1860 witnessed proportionately the heaviest immigration in American history, about fifteen percent of the host population. New Orleans was the gateway to Middle America. Some two million immigrants passed through her port en route to St. Louis and points north. But approximately 50,000, and probably more, threw down roots in the Crescent City. By 1860 New Orleans could lay claim to being the nation's preeminent melting pot city, not only by dint of numbers but the compression of geography. The river's natural levee left scant room for the European newcomers to retreat into discrete ethnic enclaves. They were thrown together—even in the so-called Irish Channel, where an Irish Catholic church and a German Catholic church still gaze at each other across a street not much wider than an alley. When you layer in the multitudes of Greeks and Sardinians, Portugese and Sicilians who dribbled into New Orleans around the same time, it is easy to see why so many travelers from abroad regarded antebellum New Orleans as one of the most cosmopolitan places on the planet.

The geographic mingling was hardly confined to the white community. The *gens de couleur libre*s, New Orleans francophone and Catholic free people of color, saw their numbers doubled by the unexpected arrival of around 10,000 Saint-Domingue exiles, approximately a third of them free blacks (and disproportionately women and children). They had been refugeeing in Cuba until Spain abruptly expelled them in 1809-10. By 1840 the Afro-Creole community had climbed above 19,000, almost one-fifth of the total population. It wasn't the South's largest free black community; Baltimore enjoyed that status. But New Orleans' free people of color comprised the most prosperous, the highest-skilled, and the best-organized community of them all. In antebellum New Orleans they formed the spine of the urban middle class. They were mechanics, shoemakers, cigar-makers, carpenters, plasterers, ironworkers, masons (an occupation they still dominate in New Orleans). They were tradesmen, retailers, barbers, boarding house keepers, hairdressers (which was Marie Laveau's trade: she ran an "advice to the lovelorn" service). Through shrewd investments in urban real estate, several accumulated modest wealth; a few amassed small fortunes. The community had sufficient means to run a school, publish a poetry journal, maintain a philharmonic society. After Emancipation, they mobilized politically behind an aggressive agenda of equal citizenship. At century's end they carried that fight all the way to the US Supreme Court in a losing effort to roll back Jim Crow segregation. (The case was called *Plessy v. Ferguson.*) America's long civil rights movement runs through this community.

Finally, there is the domestic slave trade, which, in the United States, dwarfed the African slave trade. In New Orleans, the impact was oceanic. Much of the sugar and cotton on which the city's newfound wealth rested depended on the million or so slaves who were shipped from the Upper to the Lower South in these years. Most of the transfer happened under the auspices of professional slave traders. By 1830 they had turned New Orleans into "the most busy and picturesque slave-emporium" in the country, according to an early historian of the trade. Elsewhere this human trafficking was secreted in back alleys. In New Orleans it was hidden in plain sight—near grand hotels, in Exchange Alley in the French Quarter, along Esplanade Avenue. "Slave-trading there had a peculiar dash: it rejoiced in its display and prosperity; it felt unashamed, almost proud." Those enslaved Americans were liquid capital with limbs and shrewd human intelligence. They were high-demand commodities, readily acceptable as loan collateral. As mortgaged property, they even self-financed their own sale. Simply put, they expanded the credit that built the Cotton Kingdom and irrigated the profits of much of this booming city.

The enjoyment economy that draws tourists here by the millions flowered during this hothouse period of economic transformation. Many of the restless entrepreneurs then riding the capitalist whirlwind were largely bachelors or "exiled fathers." And virtually all of them were birds of passage. At the end of the commercial season, which ran from November to May, they returned home. While sojourning in the city, if they had means, they stayed in palatial hotels like the St. Charles and the Verandah, which by day doubled as exchanges, by night as pleasure domes. ("There will be music, dancing, nonsense, eating, and flirting until three o'clock in the morning," remembered one of those extended-stay hotel residents.) The less well–to-do stayed in rooming houses. New Orleans was famed as "the boarding house of these United States." To the town's many theater impresarios, saloon keeps, and ballroom owners, this was a market desperate for an outlet. Theaters were built; the first opera in the United States was established. Gaming establishments and billiard halls sprang up on almost every corner. Dance halls and ballrooms, already numerous around the time of the Purchase, became more so, earning New Orleans a reputation as "one vast gallopading hall." There was a feverishness in how these go-getters pursued profit and pleasure. With them, it was all out, full bore, "work, work, work," even while unwinding. New Orleans' enjoyment economy seemed to function as a sort of libidinal safety valve for the constantly building pressure of chasing cotton, stocks, and inside information. They segued effortlessly from one pursuit to the other, the price current becoming an immediate topic of conversation between acts at the theater or while at table and—who knows—maybe even in the prostitution dens that were as commonplace as corner groceries. Some sort of a die was cast during these halcyon years, and there's no question its impression survives into the present.

The palatial St. Charles Hotel was the center of life in the American Sector above Canal Street for over a century. The original hotel, shown here, was designed by James Gallier Sr. and James Dakin and constructed between 1835 and 1837. It was destroyed by fire in 1851 and rebuilt a couple of years later without the dome. It, too, was destroyed by fire, in 1894. A third St. Charles Hotel was built in 1896. It stood until demolished in 1974. (Archival architectural drawing by Jim Blanchard)

Then there is the origin of jazz at the turn of the last century, not long after tens of thousands of slave-trade descendants relocated to New Orleans following Emancipation. They brought with them their field holler blues and the gospel rhythms of the sanctified church. They came into contact with musically trained Afro-Creole musicians, plus music makers of German, Irish, and Italian extraction. Jazz is the magical synthesis of a plethora of influences. It is hard to imagine—and quite futile to try—these influences fusing into a great musical vernacular in any other setting but New Orleans. She was a musical town where you could actually make money, either full-time or as a supplement to laying bricks for an income, thanks to the legacy from the good-time years before the war. And it was a place where the human diversity that still characterizes New Orleans could never retreat behind ethnic walls. That human miscellany were neighbors, often next-door neighbors. Before air conditioning, they lived outdoors, colonized their stoops of a summer evening, played ball in the street, swapped food and recipes across the backyard fence, and stole and borrowed musical licks from each other, all because Bienville's choice of site compelled them to coexist, sometimes uneasily, not to mention share a culture by building one together.

And that is one reason why New Orleans' storied past has tethered so many of her native sons and daughters to this problematic space and why our history has fostered resilience in the teeth of adversity.

The emeritus holder of the James H. Clark Endowed Chair, Lawrence N. Powell taught history at Tulane University from 1978 until his retirement in 2012. His most recent book is The Accidental City: Improvising New Orleans *(Harvard, 2012). A former Guggenheim Fellow, in 2008 he was elected as a Fellow in the Society of American Historians. In 1999, he was named Louisiana Humanist of the Year. In 2014-15 he chaired the history jury for the Pulitzer Prize.*

Acknowledgments

There were many points where the word "no" could have derailed this entire project. Fortunately, we drew all yeses.

Most important among the yea-sayers were Pelican Publishing Company President and Publisher Kathleen Calhoun Nettleton and Editor in Chief Nina Kooij, who agreed to take on the awesome responsibility of publishing this book. Their support made the project doable.

President and Chief Executive Officer Allan Pizzato provided the backing and prestige of public television station WYES, which will be a beneficiary of the project and has helped with promotions. (Thanks also to WYES's former Executive Vice President and Chief Operations Officer Beth Arroyo Utterback for her support.)

We are blessed to have the cooperation of The Historic New Orleans Collection with its treasure of art and information. Thanks to Priscilla Lawrence, the collection's Executive Director, for her support.

Our editorial staff was small but mighty. Historian John Kemp not only wrote chapters on early New Orleans history and the art scene but also provided image selection input, some captions, and first read of all articles for historical accuracy. Eve Crawford Peyton did the editing for grammar, style, and spelling. She is an expert in the field who makes sure that every comma gets its due and that no semicolon is disrespected.

Gratitude goes to the Collection's Rebecca Smith and Kevin Harrell for their assistance, as well as to WYES's Kelsi Schreiber.

There is one person who bridges all the above and then provided so much more—my wife, Peggy Scott Laborde. With her vast experience of producing books, she was able to put together the early conversations and then serve in effect as production editor, overseeing the arduous task of finding appropriate art, organizing the book, and scripting captions. More than anyone, without her this project would not exist.

Our thanks go to all those who contributed articles to the book, as well as to the production and marketing staffs of Pelican Publishing Company and WYES-TV.

Special thanks to the LeMoyne Brothers—Iberville and, especially, Bienville—who gave New Orleans its name, location, and place in history.

Most of all, thanks to you for picking up a copy of the book. May you find many discoveries within.

Originally operating from 1861-1964, the Canal Streetcar Lines (original Cemeteries and additional City Park/Museum) returned to New Orleans' "Main Street" in 2004. Instead of the traditional green color, the cars are painted red with yellow trim. The Mississippi Riverfront Streetcar and the Loyola Avenue and South Rampart–St. Claude lines are painted in the same way. (Photo by George Long)

Introduction

Books are at their best when they inspire future works, even a half century later.

Hodding Carter was a distinguished, Louisiana-born Pulitzer Prize-winning journalist and publisher who may have been best known for the fiery editorial voice that he gave to his Mississippi newspaper, the *Greenville Delta Democrat-Times*. The newspaper's pleas against racial injustice reverberated throughout the Mississippi Delta. Carter (1907-1972) wrote sixteen books and dabbled in other writing projects; one such project was a publication called *The Past as Prelude: New Orleans 1718-1968*. Carter, who at the time was writer in residence at Tulane, was editor of the book, which was published under the aegis of Tulane University. Pelican Publishing Company, which Carter owned at the time, provided "the editorial supervision and distribution."

There were fourteen chapters, each written by a distinguished expert covering a facet of the city's life in its first two and a half centuries. Journalist Pie Dufour wrote about the city's people. Political columnist Hermann Deutsch penned his essay about "New Orleans Politics—The Greatest Free Show on Earth." Carter wrote the introduction, which he opened with these magnificent sentences: "In this place the roso cane rose in a cruel thickness from the marsh and swampland. The stench of alligator musk permeated even the wheat meal, the meat and the rest of scanty provender which Canadian Pierre Le Moyne, Sieur D'Iberville, his eighteen-year-old younger brother, Jean-Baptiste Le Moyne, Sieur de Bienville, and the French and Canadian soldiers brought with them."

How many lives have been made better by this book is incalculable, but there is one for certain: me. From the moment I first discovered the publication in a library, I was mesmerized by it. Wherever I have worked, there has always been a copy nearby. It has been my urban bible, not only for its information but also for its great moments in writing, with my favorite passage being journalist and editorialist Phil Johnson's opening to a chapter headed "Good Time Town":

> Thank God the French got here first.
> Can you imagine what New Orleans might have been had the pilgrims gotten off at Pilottown instead of Plymouth?
> It's frightening . . . we might have been burning witches instead of Café Brulot; or preaching to the quadroon beauties instead of dancing with them; or spending eons eating boiled beef and potatoes, instead of Crevasses Cardinal, or Pompano en Papillote or gumbo.
> Poor pilgrims. They spent so much time merely existing that they never really learned how to live. Between fighting the Indians and fighting sin, there was little time to do anything else, and so little else for them to do.

Carter's book would go on to inspire this publication that you are holding, which attempts to honor its predecessor and, hopefully, add to the literature. Pelican Publishing has changed hands since Carter's day, but the company is still involved, serving as publisher. The book is also presented in support of public television station WYES-TV, Channel 12, with the cooperation of The Historic New Orleans Collection.

For this effort, we present twenty-one chapters reaching into contemporary times, plus essays connecting with the past, which, of course, always remains as prelude.

What the forefathers, and the fore-writers, never would have expected is that New Orleans at the time of its tricentennial really has had two histories: pre-Katrina and post-Katrina. What has happened in the after stage is as heartbreaking and as inspirational as the early story.

Obviously the Le Moyne brothers knew what they were doing when they looked for settlement sites along the river named for the late French king. In 1718, when younger brother Bienville legally established a city named after the Duc d'Orléans along a bend in the river that was flanked by lakes, he had picked a location that would be both challenged and blessed by nature. More to his concern was that it would be economically important. In 1802, Thomas Jefferson, one of a string of good writers who would wax on about the fledgling town, wrote to Robert Livingston, the US minister to France, "There is on the globe one single spot, the possessor of which is our natural and habitual enemy. It is New Orleans, through which the produce of three-eighths of our territory must pass to market, and from its fertility it will ere long yield more than half of our whole produce and contain more than half our inhabitants."

Jefferson's words took on political importance since they were advanced as part of the argument for the United States to purchase the Louisiana territory. To New Orleans' everlasting smugness, it could note that a swath of the continent, as far west as the Rockies and as far north as Canada, were thrown in as part of the deal to buy New Orleans.

Phil Johnson was right: We are fortunate that the French got here first. Napoleon Bonaparte, with other battles to fight, needed the cash, so he made the sale. The British might have held on to what they had. History takes many twists that have a powerful impact on the future. Amazingly, compared to many of the world's great cities, New Orleans is still quite young.

Three centuries later, and the adventure is just beginning.

Errol Laborde

New Orleans
The First 300 Years

LA SALLE CLAIMS THE MISSISSIPPI VALLEY FOR FRANCE.

René-Robert Cavelier, Sieur de La Salle (1643–1687), was a French explorer. He explored the Great Lakes region of the United States and Canada, the Mississippi River, and the Gulf of Mexico. La Salle claimed the entire Mississippi River basin for France. (Courtesy of The Historic New Orleans Collection)

Three Centuries in New Orleans: A Romp through Time

John R. Kemp

First Century: 1718-1818

New Orleans is a city that conjures images of a Gallic-Hispanic and Caribbean heritage in a predominantly Anglo-North American culture. Indeed, early New Orleans was very much part of that French and Spanish Caribbean world. Founded by the French on the banks of the Mississippi in 1718, ceded to Spain in 1762, regained by Napoleon in 1800, and sold to the United States in 1803, New Orleans for three centuries has survived yellow fever and cholera, fires, floods, hurricanes, revolutions, riots, booms, busts, the Civil War, Reconstruction, and Americanization with a slight Caribbean flavor.

These historic milestones began in 1682 when Robert Cavelier, Sieur de La Salle, descended from the Great Lakes to the mouth of the Mississippi, claimed the Mississippi Valley for France, and named the territory *La Louisiane* in honor of Louis XIV. He failed, however, to establish a colony. French officials eventually decided they needed a strong presence in Louisiana to block the Spanish in Florida and the British along the Atlantic seaboard. So in 1698, they dispatched an expedition headed by Canadians Pierre Le Moyne, Sieur d'Iberville, and his younger brother, Jean-Baptiste Le Moyne, Sieur de Bienville, to plant the flag. First came Biloxi, Mobile, and Natchitoches. When the decision came to establish New Orleans, Bienville wanted to build the city at its current site because it would be close to the mouth of the river and Lake Pontchartrain. Officials with the Company of the West (which had an exclusive charter to the colony) preferred a location farther upriver just below present-day Baton Rouge near the mouth of Bayou Manchac. Disregarding the company's instructions, Bienville built the city where it now stands.

Land clearing in New Orleans, so named for the French regent Philippe, Duc d'Orléans, began in spring 1718. Over the next three years, little progress was made. The town's destiny was not lost, however, on a Canadian priest who visited the village in 1721: "I have the best grounded hopes for saying that this wild and deserted place, at present almost entirely covered with canes and trees shall one day . . . become the capital of a large and rich colony. . . . Rome and Paris had not such considerable beginnings." He was right. New Orleans would become a major port, connecting the world to the upper Mississippi.

By the 1750s, New Orleans had become a pawn in a European struggle for dominance in North America. After losing the French and Indian War (Seven Years' War in Europe) to Great Britain in 1763, France ceded to Great Britain

Jean-Baptiste Le Moyne de Bienville (1680-1767) is considered the founder of New Orleans. He was born in Montreal, Canada, and was an early governor of French Louisiana, appointed four separate times between 1701 and 1743. He was a younger brother of explorer Pierre Le Moyne d'Iberville. (Courtesy of The Historic New Orleans Collection)

THE PLACE D'ARMES AT NEW ORLEANS IN THE 1730's

A sketch of New Orleans in the 1730s, where Jackson Square is today. (Courtesy of The Historic New Orleans Collection)

Canada and French territory east of the Mississippi River, keeping just two small islands in the St. Lawrence Seaway. New Orleans and Louisiana west of the river were not included. A year before, France convinced Spain to enter the war on the side of France. In return, Spain received New Orleans and Louisiana west of the river.

Spanish New Orleans was a busy place. It put down local revolts; sent supplies to American rebels during the revolution; gave refuge to Acadians driven from Nova Scotia; and settled Canary Islanders north and south of the city, where their descendants, the *Isleños*, live to this day. They also established the city's first theater, newspaper, and police force; added streetlights; and dug a canal linking the city to Bayou St. John and Lake Pontchartrain. By 1800, New Orleans had become a prosperous port with a population of almost 8,000. It also had expanded upriver into its first suburb, Faubourg Ste. Marie (1788) in today's Central Business District. Unfortunately, two fires and three hurricanes in the 1780s and 1790s destroyed much of the old French and Spanish colonial city. As a result, most buildings in the French Quarter today were constructed after the Louisiana Purchase.

As the nineteenth century began, New Orleanians were poised for another upheaval. In 1800, Napoleon forced Spain to return Louisiana to France. The news alarmed Pres. Thomas Jefferson, who wanted free navigation of the Mississippi. Hoping to avoid war with France, Jefferson offered to buy New Orleans and a portion of West Florida, including Baton Rouge. Napoleon, needing money to finance an imminent war with Great Britain and slave uprisings in Saint-Domingue, sold the entire Louisiana colony to the United States in 1803 for $15 million. Less than a decade after the purchase, new suburbs opened upriver, behind the French Quarter (Faubourg Tremé), and below Esplanade (Faubourg Marigny). It survived the 1811 slave uprising in the River Parishes and emerged as the largest city in the South, boasting a population of more than 17,000. In 1812 Louisiana became a state, and the first steamboat, the *New Orleans*, arrived in the city, launching a new era. That same year brought war with Great Britain, one that ended with an American victory at the Battle of New Orleans on January 8, 1815, in nearby Chalmette.

Second Century: 1818-1918

Thanks to sugar and cotton, the decades between the Louisiana Purchase and Civil War were mostly prosperous years in New Orleans, despite thousands of

A detail of the painting Celebrating the Louisiana Purchase, *painted by A. Karoly and L. Szantoin in 1956. The artwork was originally on view at the Missouri State Capitol and then the High Museum in Atlanta.* (From the collection of Kevin Kelly)

lives lost to yellow fever and cholera. It ranked among the wealthiest cities in the nation and was the South's largest port and slave market. It grew steadily with the arrival of Americans, immigrants from Ireland and Germany, and refugees fleeing slave rebellions in Haiti. New Orleans was a cosmopolitan city with a unique cultural blend. Its large population of free people of color, for example, was active in all aspects of commercial and cultural life. This impressed famed landscape architect Frederick Law Olmsted during his visit in the 1850s. "I doubt if there is a city in the world," he noted in his 1856 landmark book, *A Journey in the Seaboard Slave States*, "where the resident population has been so divided in its origin, or where there is such a variety in the tastes, habits, manners, and moral codes of citizens." Also during these years, Anglo-Americans edged out Creoles (descendants of colonial New Orleanians) for dominance in city politics and commerce. Right up to the Civil War, local political campaigns often triggered bloody riots among immigrants, Creoles, and anti-foreigner nativists.

By 1860, thoughts turned to the election of Abraham Lincoln and war. To many New Orleanians with strong business ties to the North, secession in January 1861 seemed illogical. That inconvenience ended in April 1862 when the city fell to Union forces commanded by Adm. David Farragut. First up was Maj. Gen. Benjamin Butler, a retired Massachusetts politician, who took command in May 1862. Locals tagged him "Beast Butler" or "Spoons Butler" because of the huge amounts of property his subordinates confiscated from

Beginning in 1831 and continuing for a little over a century, the Pontchartrain Railroad ran down Elysian Fields from Lake Pontchartrain to the Mississippi River. Locals referred to what eventually became a steam train line as the Smoky Mary. While initially used for linking commerce, it eventually provided transportation for travelers and for visitors to the Milneburg Resort. (Courtesy of The Historic New Orleans Collection)

The Krewe of Orpheus parade includes a signature float in tribute to the famed Smoky Mary train, which travelled down Elysian Fields Avenue from Lake Pontchartrain to the back of the French Quarter. (Photo by Peggy Scott Laborde)

Gallier Hall, located on Lafayette Square, was constructed between 1845 and 1853. Built as a city hall, it is considered one of America's finest examples of Greek Revival architecture and a hallmark of the career of architect James Gallier. It was designated a National Historic Landmark in 1974. Today it continues to be used for city-related and special events. (Archival drawing by James Blanchard)

Gallier Hall in the twenty-first century, restored and illuminated for the Mardi Gras season. (Photo by Peggy Scott Laborde)

"unreconstructed" local inhabitants. And then came his notorious General Order No. 28 that said any woman who harassed union soldiers would be treated as a "woman of the town plying her avocation." Historians, however, are kinder to Butler. He fed the poor, financed orphanages, reorganized public schools, and hired thousands of white and black residents for city improvement projects.

Though the war ended in 1865, Reconstruction in New Orleans witnessed several violent attempts by local Democrats to seize state government from Republicans, despite efforts by more conciliatory New Orleanians to unify the city. In addition, the corrupt Louisiana State Lottery Company (1868-1894) reached into every aspect of the city's Gilded Age politics. But not all was gloomy during Reconstruction, which ended in April 1877. African Americans gained many rights as citizens. Theaters and operas played to large audiences. Boxing, baseball, and horse and riverboat racing drew big crowds. The arts flourished, and Carnival became even grander with the arrival of Rex in 1872.

For the remainder of the century, New Orleans witnessed a fluctuating economy and more demographic changes. Before the war, immigrants were mostly Irish and Germans. Now came former slaves from plantations and poor Sicilians. New Orleans was still the South's largest city, and boosters promoted it with events such as the World's Industrial and Cotton Centennial Exposition of 1884-1885, an ambitious effort to showcase local arts and industry to the world. Though a financial failure, it helped develop Audubon Park and uptown New Orleans.

A new image of New Orleans also emerged during these years. Writers such as Grace King, George Washington Cable, and Charles Gayarré created a romantic Old New Orleans mythology that lives on to this day.

But there was a dark side. In 1891 mobs lynched more than a dozen Sicilians held in jail for the murder of police chief David Hennessy. In addition, African American hopes for equal rights were dashed in the 1890s when Homer Plessy, a local African American, challenged the state's segregation laws by sitting in a railway car reserved for whites. His case ended with the 1896 US Supreme Court decision *Plessy v. Ferguson*, making segregation the law of the land until it was overturned in 1954 by *Brown v. Board of Education of Topeka*. And then in 1900 there was the Robert Charles race riot that ended in the death of Charles, a member of a back-to-Africa movement, and more than a dozen white and black citizens.

During these years, the city expanded further uptown, downriver, on the West Bank, and out toward the lake. Skyscrapers rose above Canal Street, and jazz was born in the saloons and brothels of Storyville, South Rampart Street, and along the lakefront. With reforms begun in the late 1890s by Mayor Walter Flower and continued by his successors Paul Capdevielle and Martin Behrman, the city built new drainage and sewerage systems and a public belt railroad; paved streets; and constructed a modern water purification plant to replace private rainwater cisterns, a breeding place for yellow fever-bearing mosquitoes. As a result, the city suffered its last yellow fever epidemic in 1905.

Union general Benjamin Butler governed the city of New Orleans with an iron fist during the early days of Reconstruction. He was very unpopular in the community but is credited for doing much to improve the city's sanitation problems. (From the collection of Peggy Scott Laborde)

THE WORLD'S INDUSTRIAL & COTTON CENTENNIAL EXPOSITION.

OPEN DEC. 1ST 1884 TO MAY. 31ST 1885

NEW ORLEANS

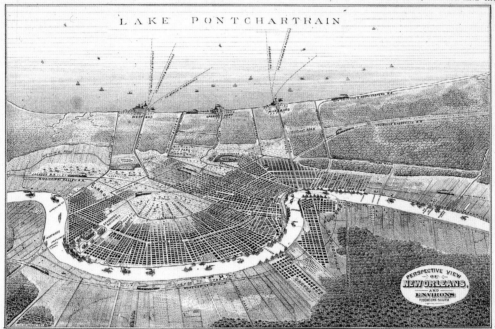

THE MAIN BUILDING---1378x905 feet.

UNITED STATES AND STATE EXHIBITS 885x565 feet.

NATIONAL AND INTERNATIONAL.

AN EXPOSITION OF THE WORLD'S

COMMERCE, INDUSTRY, MECHANICS, EDUCATION, AGRICULTURE, HORTICULTURE, LIVE STOCK, PISCICULTURE, SCIENCE AND ART.

LAKE PONTCHARTRAIN

PERSPECTIVE VIEW OF NEW ORLEANS, AND ENVIRONS FROM THE SOUTH

FACTORIES AND MILLS 350x120 FEET.

HORTICULTURAL HALL, 600x194 FEET.

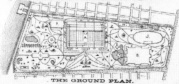

THE GROUND PLAN.

SCALE 1430 FEET TO THE INCH.

A—Main Building.   E—Art Gallery.   I—Grand Fountain, eighty feet high.
B—U. S. and State Exhibits.   F—Factories and Mills.   J—Live Stock Arena.
C—Horticultural Hall.   G—Live Stock Stables, etc.,   K—Saw Mills and Woodworking Machinery.
D—Mexican Buildings.   H—Storage.   L—Wharf, Mississippi River.

The grounds embrace the space of 247 acres, bounded on the north side by St. Charles Avenue, on the south by the Mississippi. The buildings front east towards the main portion of the city.
An electric railway encircles the grounds.

FACTORIES AND MILLS 350x120 FEET.

EXHIBITS.

Beside the States and Territories of this country, which will be fully represented, a large number of foreign countries have arranged for imposing exhibits—notably, China, Japan and Siam, and on this continent, the United States of Mexico. The latter country is erecting two large structures of special design and very attractive architecture, beside laying out into a tropical garden a five-acre tract of ground.

STRUCTURES.

Beside the buildings here represented, there will be numerous others. Many of the States will erect special buildings for headquarters and reception. An extensive range of buildings is being erected for the housing and display of live stock. A large building to accommodate several complete saw and planing mills is located on the grounds near to the river bank. Several smaller buildings for various purposes will be required.

TRANSPORTATION.

Nearly every transportation line in the United States has made a reduction of one-half in the rates on all articles designed for exhibit. A number of lines have agreed to forward without charge.

The reduction agreed to by nearly all leading railways in passenger fares is very large—much greater than ever secured for similar purposes. Full and detailed information concerning passenger rates will be furnished in ample time.

ACCOMMODATION.

Arrangements for the accommodation of visitors, being made by the Department of Information and Accommodation, will assure the public certainty in securing comfortable entertainment at reasonable rates. The facilities of New Orleans for this purpose will be found ample.

Special information upon any subject pertaining to the Exposition will be promptly furnished by addressing E. A. BURKE, Director General, New Orleans.

The World's Industrial and Cotton Centennial Exposition, 1884-1885. Located on the site of today's Audubon Park, the Cotton Centennial Exposition was an ambitious effort to showcase Louisiana arts and industry to the world. Though financially unsuccessful, it helped develop Uptown New Orleans. (Lithograph by Henry W.W. Reynolds, lithograph, ca. 1884. Courtesy of The Historic New Orleans Collection.)

The 1984 Louisiana World Exposition, also known as the World's Fair, was located along the Mississippi Riverfront and contributed to the transformation of the Warehouse District in New Orleans. (Photo © by Mitchel Osborne)

A cabinet card of a New Orleanian around the turn of the twentieth century. (Photograph by Myers Studio. From the collection of Peggy Scott Laborde.)

Three young ladies who are probably sisters sat for a photograph by New Orleans photographer Frank J. Barnes around the turn of the twentieth century. (From the collection of Peggy Scott Laborde)

This cabinet card is of a New Orleanian in the early 1900s. (Photo by the L. Gugliemi Studios. From the collection of Peggy Scott Laborde.)

Third Century: 1918-Present

Sadly, New Orleans, now home to the gin fizz, hot music, and tolerant lifestyles, began a slow economic decline after Reconstruction. With the growth of manufacturing in other parts of the country and the emergence of a national network of railroads and later trucking, cities such as Atlanta grew rapidly while New Orleans, whose selling point was river cargo and light industry, dropped from the ninth largest city in 1870 to the twelfth in 1900 and to the seventeenth by 1920. Yet the decades between World War I and World War II were transformative years. The French Quarter became a bohemia for artists and writers. The city closed the red-light district Storyville, built the Industrial Canal and public housing, beautified the lakefront, and survived the 1927 flood and streetcar strike of 1929. New Deal agencies renovated historic architecture and constructed new public buildings such as Charity Hospital. World War II brought thousands of jobs, especially in building the famous Higgins landing craft and torpedo boats that put millions of troops on beaches from Normandy to Saipan.

During the 1960s, 1970s, and 1980s, after the heady post-war years of Mayor deLesseps "Chep" Morrison (1946-1961), the city again experienced tectonic social shifts. School desegregation, rising urban crime, and new expressways led to a mass outmigration of many middle-class white and black families to the suburbs, leaving behind a decaying inner city. Yet many who remained created organizations such as the Preservation Resource Center to protect historic architecture and neighborhoods. With thousands of families now settled in new suburbs, the city's population fell from about 620,000 in 1960 to a little more than 550,000 in 1980. This outmigration enabled the rise of African American political organizations and the election of the city's first black mayor, Ernest "Dutch" Morial (1978-1986). Meanwhile, a new wave of immigrants—Cubans and Vietnamese—arrived in the city to add to the local cultural mix. During those same years, the city suffered four disasters and two major controversies: Hurricane Betsy (1965), the ill-fated Riverfront Expressway (1969), the Rault Center fire (1972), sniper Mark Essex (1972), the Upstairs Lounge fire (1973), and the New Orleans police strike (1979). On the economic side, the city did well thanks to tourism, the port, NASA's space program at Michoud, and petrochemical industries. The new Louisiana Superdome and glitzy high-rises towered over the skyline, and the 1984 Louisiana World Exposition opened with fanfare. Suddenly, the bubble burst with the 1986 oil bust.

Within a decade, however, petroleum was back and tourism became a $5 billion-plus industry. Good times were ahead, or so everyone thought. Then on August 29, 2005, Hurricane Katrina slammed Louisiana and Mississippi's Gulf Coast. The world watched as New Orleans drowned in putrid floodwaters when its floodwalls failed. Hundreds died, and thousands of homes were destroyed. Within weeks, the city's population plummeted from approximately 485,000 to 144,000. There were upsides to the slow and painful recovery, however. The New Orleans Saints won the Super Bowl in February 2010 (a miracle), the city got a new flood protection system, and the Central Business District experienced a building boom that included a new LSU-VA medical complex. Moreover, young people from across the nation, hyped by post-Katrina publicity, moved to New Orleans to give new life to old neighborhoods and the economy. By 2015, the population was back up to about 389,000. Unfortunately, the conviction of former mayor C. Ray Nagin (2002-2010) on corruption charges a year earlier tainted a cautious optimism that permeated the city.

Though poverty and crime continue to haunt New Orleans, a renaissance is underway as the city approaches its tricentennial. After three centuries, New Orleans remains a city like no other. Novelist James Lee Burke captured that spirit in a post-Katrina story for *Esquire* magazine—"New Orleans was a poem, man, a song in your heart that never died."

John R. Kemp has written, edited, and contributed chapters for seventeen books on Louisiana art and history, including New Orleans: An Illustrated History, Martin Behrman of New Orleans: Memoirs of a City Boss, Louisiana's Black Heritage *(coeditor),* The Uniting States: The Story of Statehood for the Fifty United States of America, Expressions of Place: The Contemporary Louisiana Landscape, *and* A Unique Slant of Light: The Bicentennial History of Art in Louisiana *(coeditor). He also writes about Southern artists for regional and national magazines, including* Louisiana Life *and the New York-based* ARTnews, *and covers New Orleans art for the WYES show* Steppin' Out.

Ursuline nuns arrived in New Orleans from France on August, 7, 1727. During those early years, the order operated orphanages, a hospital, a pharmacy, and a school for girls, which continues to this day. The Ursuline Convent on Chartres St., completed in 1753, reportedly is the only building in the French Quarter to survive from the French colonial era. (Hermitage Art, circa 1930. Courtesy of The Historic New Orleans Collection.)

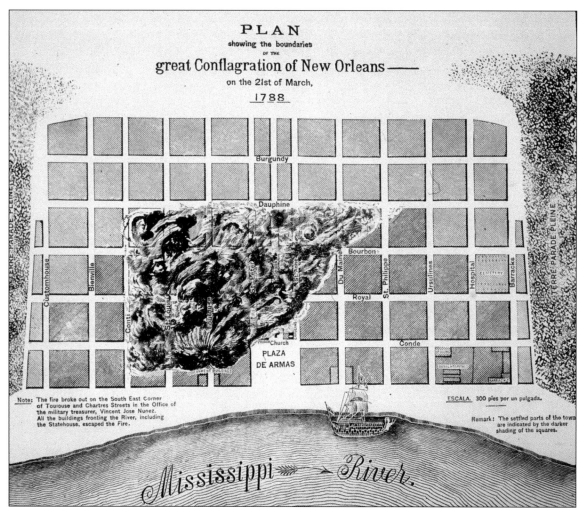

"Boundaries of the Great Conflagration of New Orleans on the 21st March 1788" illustrates the vast damage caused by the fire that swept the early city on the morning of Good Friday 1788. Almost 80 percent of the city was left in ashes. (Courtesy of The Historic New Orleans Collection)

Evolution from a Complex Heritage

Robert Cangelosi, Jr.

Ask anyone what he or she thinks of when describing New Orleans, and architecture will be on the list. New Orleans' architectural legacy is rich, resulting from its distinctive heritage. As the city was founded by French Canadians, New Orleans' initial architecture was influenced by Canadian and French building traditions but was adapted for a completely different climate. The 1745 Ursuline Convent on Chartres Street is the city's sole surviving building from the French colonial period. Its design was inspired by the French military design book *La Science des Ingenieurs*, published in Paris in 1729.

Gradually, more appropriate building elements, such as galleries, were added to the initial French core and houses were raised on a *rez de chaussée* (ground floor)—a characteristic lasting until World War II and now known as "basements." French colonies in the Caribbean, Canada, and Africa followed similar evolutions.

Spanish dominion changed little of New Orleans' architectural vocabulary. Two major eighteenth-century fires destroyed much of the city's colonial architecture; consequently, less than forty Spanish-era buildings survive. A 1795 building code attempted to stop the spread of such disastrous fires. As the city urbanized, the Creole cottage and the shop residence were introduced. Surviving Spanish Colonial-era buildings include Madame John's Legacy (1789) and the Cabildo (1799).

Through the encouragement of Spanish officials, Americans started to immigrate into the city, and following the 1803 Louisiana Purchase, a flood of Americans poured in. Architect Benjamin Latrobe wrote: "I have no doubt but that the American style [of architecture] will ultimately be that of the whole city." Latrobe was correct. Architectural taste changed quickly as architects and builders previously practicing in the North came to the city with new ideas.

Americans initially sought inspiration from the ancient Roman republic as the fledgling country broke with English tradition. They introduced the Federal style (1803-1840) to New Orleans, typified by the Hermann-Grima House (1831), designed by Virginia-born William Brand. This house would be quite at home in any eastern seaboard city. The largest percentage of surviving Vieux Carré buildings date from this early American period. Because New Orleans is a port city with no natural stone and poor local bricks, building products and ideas were imported from the east coast and European ports as cotton and sugar were exported.

The Hermann-Grima House is an example of the Federal style of architecture, which America introduced after the Louisiana Purchase in 1803. (Courtesy of the Hermann-Grima/Gallier Historic Houses)

Madame John's Legacy, located at 632 Dumaine Street in the historic New Orleans French Quarter, is one of the finest examples of eighteenth-century Creole colonial architecture in the Lower Mississippi River Valley and North America. Its popular name is taken from New Orleans native George Washington Cable's 1874 fictional short story "'Tite Poulette." It is now part of the Louisiana State Museum system. (Courtesy of the Louisiana State Museum)

Following the Federal style, New Orleans, like the rest of the nation, saw numerous revival styles during the nineteenth and early twentieth centuries, among them the Greek Revival (1830-1850); the Romanesque Revival (1850-1920) and its variant form, the Richardsonian Romanesque (1880-1910), developed by Louisiana native Henry Hobson Richardson; the Colonial Revival in all its variations (1885-1940); the Tudor Revival (1890-1935); the Gothic Revival (1835-1940); and the Renaissance Revival (1850-1930). The Italianate (1840-1880), Second Empire (1860-1890), Mediterranean (1900-1935), French Eclectic (1920-1945), and Exotic styles (1930-1940) complemented the eclectic carnival of styles borrowed from the past.

The Italianate style was nationally promoted by architectural pattern books. Its primary inspiration came from picturesque Italian farmhouses in the Tuscany region, as the style attempted to break from the symmetry and classicism of the Greek Revival style. The Italianate's greatest impact locally was the use of cast iron. Primarily manufactured in the North, it was popular especially for verandas, which were often used to modernize older buildings such as those in the Vieux Carré. A vernacular form of the Italianate style was commonly employed for the city's working-class residences, known as "shotguns." This house type's origins are greatly debated, and they can be found in numerous neighborhoods in picturesque rows.

Designed by Gilberto Guillemard, the Cabildo got its name for the Spanish municipal council, or Cabildo, that met within its walls. Built between 1795 and 1799 after the Great Fire of 1788, architectural historians believe the locally made wrought-iron balcony rails are the finest examples of ironwork from the Spanish colonial era. The American emblem in the building's pediment, added in 1821, was the work of Italian sculptor Pierre Cardelli. The Mansard roof was added in 1847. The Louisiana Purchase transfer ceremony from France to the United States took place in the second floor Sala Capitular in 1803. (Photo by Jay Rosenblatt. Courtesy of the Louisiana State Museum)

The late nineteenth century's Aesthetic movement brought to New Orleans the picturesque Queen Anne (1880-1910) and Eastlake (1880-1910) styles. A guidebook for the 1884 Cotton Centennial stated that all of the new houses in the city along its major avenues were built in the Queen Anne style. St. Charles was the grand avenue for showcasing this Victorian style. While upper- and middle-class housing employed the Queen Anne style, the Eastlake style was common for middle- and low-income housing. The two styles are contemporary with each other and share common characteristics.

During Reconstruction, Northern capital plundered Southern forests, and thousands of board feet of lumber were shipped out of Gulf Coast ports as dimensional lumber, architectural features, and mass-produced houses. In New Orleans, Roberts and Company produced and sold a wealth of details and entire houses in late-nineteenth-century styles.

The twentieth century's Arts and Crafts movement introduced several architectural styles with shared characteristics. These styles are commonly associated with the bungalow house and, later, the ranch house. They include the California (1905-1935), Craftsman (1905-1935), Decorative Brick (1905-1935), Prairie (1910-1920), and Taliesin (1935-1965) styles. Mass-produced houses continued to be popular and promoted by such groups as the Southern Pine and Cypress Associations, Sears and Roebuck, and Montgomery Ward. Neighborhoods such as Gentilly and Lakeview developed during this period. Architect Albert Ledner, a student of Frank Lloyd Wright, produced Taliesin designs such as the Unitarian Church (1955) and the Sunkel residence (1962).

The French Quarter's legendary courtyards grew out of a twentieth-century preservation movement that transformed functional yards and rebranded the French Quarter as Spanish. This courtyard is located in the rear of Antiques De Provence on Royal Street. (Photo by Peggy Scott Laborde)

The twentieth century also saw a full-blown preservation movement, as the city and the private sector worked together to preserve New Orleans' architectural heritage. City leaders saw tourism as a boost to an economy that had floundered since the Civil War; they joined with preservationists to promote a largely intact architectural legacy that would not be destroyed by either the Civil War or an economic boom that fostered replacement of older buildings. The local chapter of the American Institute of Architects (AIA) was a pioneer in the city's preservation efforts. They worked for the formation of the Vieux Carré Commission and funded and staffed many preservation initiatives. In an attempt to promote the Vieux Carré's preservation, it was rebranded as Spanish, as the Spanish Eclectic movement was sweeping the country. American cast iron was misidentified as Spanish wrought iron, and the yards of the buildings were redesigned as Spanish courtyards with fountains and raised flower beds, following the lead of local architect Richard Koch, who based his work on the courtyards of Spain.

The Historic American Building Survey, established in 1933 and run locally by Koch, documented many city landmarks. In 1956, the Louisiana Landmarks Society was formed to save local landmarks after the Mississippi River Bridge construction destroyed many in its path. The Friends of the Cabildo began publishing its New Orleans architecture series in 1971, documenting the city's architectural legacy. And as an outgrowth of the Friends' Building Watchers tours, the Preservation Resource Center was founded in 1974. Legislation in 1975 enabled the city to establish the Historic District and Landmarks Commission, which currently oversees 14 historic districts and 297 landmarks.

Southern Railway Terminal (1908-1956). Located at Basin and Canal Streets, the terminal sat at the entrance to the city's infamous tenderloin district, Storyville. Designed by Chicago's famed architect Daniel Burnham, the station was demolished by the city in 1956 with the opening of the new Union Passenger Terminal on Loyola Avenue. (Photograph ca. 1916-1925 by Charles L. Franck Photographers. Reprinted between 1979 and 1983. Courtesy of The Historic New Orleans Collection.)

John Lawrence, dean of Tulane's Architecture School, wrote in the 1957 AIA guidebook: "To build almost anywhere in New Orleans poses the problem of placing the new with the old, if not literally, then at least in spirit. . . . Thus it becomes a particular responsibility of contemporary New Orleans architecture to prove that the new can live graciously with the old and that the new can become graciously old; there must be a more mature concern with the *toute ensemble* and for the enrichment of a valid tradition."

The twentieth-century Modern movement brought the Art Nouveau (1900-1920), International (1925-1927), Art Deco (1920-1940), Streamline Moderne (1927-1940), Mid-Century Modern (1945-1965), New Formalism (1960-1980), Post-Modern (1965-present), Neo-Eclecticism (1965-present), and styles popular just before and after Hurricane Katrina (2005).

Architect H. Jordan Mackenzie, after seeing the German Pavilion at the 1904 St. Louis Louisiana Purchase Exposition, brought Art Nouveau to New Orleans architecture. Newcomb pottery had already established a taste for the style in the city's decorative arts. Mackenzie's local work was inspired by Austrian architect Josef Olbrich, a leader in the Austrian Art Nouveau, or Secessionist, movement. Mackenzie's residence on West End Boulevard—with its bright blue roof—earned him the nickname "Blue Roof Mackenzie."

New Orleans had a small Art Deco district downtown with film studios such as Fox and Warner Brothers and the Tulane, LSU, and Charity medical complexes. Other noteworthy buildings around town include Shushan Airport (1934) and the General Laundry Building (1929). Art Deco's geometric shapes were a reaction to the fluid Art Nouveau shapes.

Industrial designers such as Raymond Lowey helped to bring the Streamline Moderne, with its slick curved shapes, to New Orleans. Lowey designed the city's now-demolished Greyhound Bus station on Canal Street (1935). Local architects contributed such designs as the Blue Plate building (1941) on Jefferson Davis Parkway and the Lake Vista Center (1950).

The initial phase of the International style had little impact in New Orleans, but by mid-century, it had a more significant one. Some designs blended Taliesin's Arts and Crafts influences with the International style's functional aesthetic, such as in St. James Major (1955) and Grace Episcopal (1956) Churches. Blended residences include the Harry Batt (1955) and Louis Roussel (1957) residences on the Lakefront. Other mid-century designs more closely follow the initial principles of the style—balance rather than symmetry, volume rather than mass, and a prohibition of applied ornamentation. The international architectural firm of Skidmore, Owen, and Merrill gave New Orleans the Pan American Insurance Building (1952) on Canal Street and the John Hancock Building (1963) on St. Charles Avenue. The local firm of Curtis and Davis designed such buildings as the Jewish Community Center (1961) and Thomy Lafon Elementary School (1954), and Charles Colbert was the architect for the now-demolished Phillis Wheatley Elementary School (1954).

The mid-twentieth century gave New Orleans a new governmental complex downtown (1956-1959) with City Hall, civil district courts, a library, and a now-demolished state building and, in Mid-City, the police complex (1966-1968). There were a handful of Mid-Century Modern residences such as the Kirschmann (1962) and Curtis (1962) residences.

Post-mid-century architecture introduced a diversity of modern styles incorporating numerous ideas and concepts. Neo-Expressionism designs with complex forms include the now-demolished St. Francis Xavier Cabrini Catholic Church (1963) and Rivergate Convention Center (1968). New Formalism took a Beaux Arts approach to design but employed a contemporary vocabulary and gave the city St. Raphael the Archangel Catholic Church (1958), Whitney Bank (1966), and the Auto Life Building (1963). Post-Modernism's whimsy rejected the "less is more" and "form follows function" philosophy of the International style. Products of this style include the Piazza d'Italia (1978), the Louisiana World Exposition's Wonderwall (1984), and Xavier University's science building (1999).

The oil boom of the 1970s and early 1980s added skyscrapers to New Orleans' skyline with One Shell Square (1972) and Place St. Charles (1984). The late 1980s and 1990s were a soft period for new architecture in New Orleans as the city capitalized on its architectural legacy. Developers, especially downtown, took advantage of the 1976 Tax Reform Act, contracting numerous historic tax credit rehabilitations. Among the larger conversion projects were the Federal Fibre Mills Building (1985) and Woodward Wight (1999). Notable restoration projects of the period include the Cabildo in Jackson Square following a 1988 fire.

Changes in the field, such as computer-aided architectural design (CAAD) programs, have had their impact on local architecture. CAAD software was used for buildings dating from the 1970s, such as the Superdome and One Shell Square, but in the years just before and after Hurricane Katrina, it dominated the profession. The designs of University Medical Center (2015), Landry-Walker High School (2010), and 930 Poydras (2010) clearly demonstrate the computer's impact. Sustainable architecture has also become the norm, as the state passed a requirement that new construction meet a minimum energy conservation standard. Because of low energy prices and a loss of regionalism, Mid-Century Modern buildings consumed high levels of energy. The Make It Right projects in the Lower Ninth Ward and Tulane's URBANbuild housing projects throughout town are all designed to LEED (Leadership in Energy and Environmental Design) standards.

Although Hurricane Katrina did a tremendous amount of damage to the city, FEMA had to adhere to the 1966 Preservation Act, which required historic facilities (those older than fifty years) to be repaired rather than replaced when possible. Hospitals, such as the Veterans Affairs Hospital (2017), and schools, such as the Mary D. Coghill Elementary School (2014), were the principal types of buildings constructed post-Katrina. For the most part, the city's housing stock was renovated with Road Home grants. In hard-hit areas like Lakeview, new housing was built—much of which was eclectic in style, as homes have been since World War II. Many existing houses were elevated to meet the city's base flood elevations, and new houses were built to strict hurricane-code compliance.

New Orleans' future architectural challenge is to add to its legacy while complementing and preserving it.

Robert J. Cangelosi Jr., AIA, is president of Koch and Wilson Architects. His practice has focused on the preservation of hundreds of historic structures. He has served as a coauthor and contributor to several architectural books. Cangelosi teaches New Orleans architecture at Tulane University. He serves on the New Orleans Central Business District Historic District Landmarks Commission architectural review committee and on numerous preservation boards. He holds a bachelor's and a master's degree in architecture, interned at National Trust for Historic Preservation, and attended the Preservation Institute: Nantucket.

The Degas House, 2306 Esplanade Avenue, was the home of the Musson Family, cousins to French Impressionist Hilaire-German Edgar Degas. The painter came to New Orleans for a five-month stay with the Mussons in the fall and spring of 1872 and 1873. The building is a bed and breakfast and open for tours and special events. (Photo by Peggy Scott Laborde)

Transformations in the
Changing Light

John R. Kemp

New Orleans and its surrounding landscape have inspired artists for generations. Whether it is the land, culture, or people, artists are drawn to the city's collective memory and experience.

Novelist Walker Percy, who lived in the New Orleans area for many years, described the city as an island "cut adrift not only from the South but from the rest of Louisiana, somewhat like Mont Saint-Michel awash at high tide."

Looking back, the arts have thrived on Percy's island since the mid-nineteenth century, when New Orleans ranked among the wealthiest cities in the nation. Before the Civil War, portrait painting ruled. By the end of Reconstruction in 1877, the city's visual art scene entered a golden age. The transcendental Hudson River school and realism of the Barbizon painters dominated the New Orleans art world in the late nineteenth century. The most influential of these painters was the Paris-born Louisiana artist Richard Clague Jr., followed by a number of others whose landscape paintings now grace the best art collections.

The most acclaimed artist to see the visual possibilities of New Orleans was the French impressionist Hilaire-Germain-Edgar Degas, who spent the fall and spring of 1872 and 1873 in the city, visiting his American relatives. His mother, Marie-Célestine Musson Degas, was a member of an old French Creole family. Everything he saw fascinated him—the people, machinery, and marketplaces. In a letter home to a friend, Degas wrote: "I am accumulating plans which would take ten lifetimes to carry out." Unfortunately, he spent most of his time sketching family members, including a portrait of his cousin and sister-in-law, Estelle, which now hangs in the New Orleans Museum of Art (NOMA). The outside light was too intense for his failing vision. His most acclaimed painting from this visit was *A Cotton Office in New Orleans* (1873).

As in the rest of the nation, the visual arts in New Orleans underwent many transformations between the 1880s and World War II, thanks mainly to newly formed art associations and institutions. In the mid-1880s, for instance, the World's Industrial and Cotton Centennial Exposition, held on the site of today's Audubon Park, promoted local artists to the world while exposing locals to art from other countries. Also, Tulane University hired William and Ellsworth Woodward of Massachusetts to teach art at Tulane and the new Newcomb College. Both were painters steeped in the Arts and Crafts movement and impressionism, and both influenced subsequent generations of artists. Newcomb pottery is one of their legacies. Prominent artists also created the Southern Art Union in 1880; its successor, the Artists' Association of New Orleans in 1886;

Edgar Degas, Portrait of Estelle Musson Degas. *Estelle was the cousin and sister-in-law of Edgar Degas. Estelle, who went blind at an early age, married Edgar's brother René, who later abandoned his wife and returned to France where he remarried. The New Orleans Museum of Art purchased the portrait in the 1960s.* (Courtesy of The New Orleans Museum of Art: Museum purchase through Public Subscription, 65.1.)

The New Orleans Museum of Art, situated in City Park, is the city's oldest fine arts museum. Founded as the Delgado Museum of Art (named after philanthropist Isaac Delgado), it opened in 1911. (Photo by Peggy Scott Laborde)

Ellsworth Woodward established the pottery program at Newcomb College of Art in 1895, at the height of the Arts and Crafts Movement. With succeeding generations of female student designers, Newcomb Pottery and its varying artistic styles quickly gained international acclaim. (Courtesy of The Historic New Orleans Collection)

Glazed ceramic vase with Espanol design, 1928, by Anna Frances Simpson (1880-1930). (Courtesy of The Historic New Orleans Collection)

William Woodward pastel of a French Quarter scene. (Courtesy of The Historic New Orleans Collection)

and Delgado Museum of Art (now NOMA) in 1911. Later, in 1921, Alberta Kinsey and a small group of painters formed the Arts and Crafts Club of New Orleans as a "counterbalance to some of the more conservative tendencies of the Delgado Museum." These artists, continued art historian Estill Pennington, were less interested in the more radical art movements coming from Europe than they were in the "caricaturish satiric style" that influenced artists such as Caroline Durieux and regionalist painter John McCrady. Then came the New Orleans Art League in 1927, which for decades provided studio and exhibit space for prominent local artists.

From the 1920s and well into the 1970s, New Orleans had become, in Tennessee Williams' words, "the last frontier of Bohemia." It attracted modernist painters and sculptors such as the Paris-trained Juan José Calandria and his wife, Challis Walker Calandria; Paul Ninas, who settled in the city in 1932; and longtime Newcomb College art professor Will Henry Stevens, whom art historian Richard Gruber described as a "visionary modernist" and "pioneer in the field of Southern art." Though European-inspired modernism had proponents in New Orleans, most local artists in the 1920s and 1930s continued to paint impressionistic landscapes and still lifes while others worked in the emerging American scene, or regionalism, movement. This new style thrived in New Orleans during the Depression as a result of Huey Long's ambitious construction projects, such as the "new" state capitol in Baton Rouge, and programs initiated by the Federal Art Project under the Works Progress Administration. In post offices, hospitals, libraries, courthouses, schools, and parks across the state, artists such as McCrady, Ninas, Conrad Albrizio, Enrique Alférez, Xavier Gonzales, and Angela Gregory left a legacy of murals and sculpted works glorifying the state's agriculture, culture, history, and industries. After World War II and into the 1950s and 1960s, American scene painting gave way to an array of new styles, such as abstract expressionism, minimalism, and op art. In New Orleans, that contemporary art world revolved around local college art departments, as well as the Arts and Crafts Club (later known as the Arts and Crafts Gallery) plus the Downtown Gallery and Galerie Simonne Stern. Meanwhile, throughout the last half of the twentieth century, college art professors developed their own artistic voices in the various post-war contemporary art movements while mentoring younger generations of artists. On the more conservative side, private art schools, such as those run by the Calandrias, McCrady, and Charles Reinike, turned out students trained in more traditional approaches to painting.

Beginning in the late 1960s, a new generation of cultural activists, art collectors, and artists emerged with fresh creative energy. In 1976, a group of them formed the Contemporary Arts Center (CAC) to expose the public to new ideas and voices. Equally important, the CAC and the 1984 New Orleans World's Fair were catalysts in turning the decaying warehouse neighborhood, especially along Julia Street, into today's Arts District with first-rate galleries. Later, in 1999, came the Ogden Museum of Southern Art with its mission to give Southern art its due. Focusing on black artists, the Ashé Cultural Arts Center opened in 1998 in Central City, followed two years later by the New Orleans African American Museum of Art, Culture and

Water Goddess, *1930s, was one of many sculptures and artworks created for City Park during the Great Depression by the acclaimed Mexican-born New Orleans sculptor Enrique Alférez. (Photo by Peggy Scott Laborde)*

Terminal of the New Orleans Lakefront Airport. It was originally named Shushan Airport for longtime Orleans Levee Board President Abraham "Abe" Shushan. The facility was renamed New Orleans Airport in 1939 after Shushan was implicated in the widespread political "Louisiana Scandals" of the late 1930s. Enrique Alferez designed all of the bas-relief work for the exterior and interior of the airport terminal. (Photo by John R. Kemp)

History in Tremé. In 2007, the George and Leah McKenna Museum of African American Art gave even greater depth to the Central City art scene. NOMA also expanded twice and, in 2003, added its impressive Sydney and Walda Besthoff Sculpture Garden. To train school-age children and teens in the arts, two organizations emerged: the New Orleans Center for Creative Arts (NOCCA) in 1973 and YAYA in 1988. Equally important, new galleries in the Arts District, French Quarter, and along Magazine Street and St. Claude Avenue were indispensible in promoting local artists. At the other end of the art spectrum stood the New Orleans Academy of Fine Arts, founded in 1978 by artist Auseklis Ozols to give students a more classical training in art techniques. Not to ignore the past, The Historic New Orleans Collection (THNOC), Louisiana State Museum, NOMA, and the Ogden continuously organized exhibits featuring prominent local artists as well as historic New Orleans art. The city is not likely to forget NOMA's wildly popular blockbusters *Treasures of Tutankhamun* in 1977-1978 and *Monet: Late Paintings of Giverny* in 1995. On the economic side, the Arts Council of New Orleans, created in 1975 and expanded in 1981, stimulated the art market through grants to artists and the purchase of artwork for public spaces. In addition, commercial publishers and university presses gave artists of all stripes even greater public exposure.

Thanks to these institutions and dramatic growth in the city's art scene, art in New Orleans has gained national stature while traveling in aesthetic and

The Contemporary Arts Center, 900 Camp Street, is an arts complex located in the historic Arts (Warehouse) District. Founded in 1976, the center showcases the visual arts and is also a venue for the performing arts. (Photo by Frank Aymami III)

intellectual directions, ranging from the traditional to the symbolic to the totally abstract. It has been an era of vibrant artistic and stylistic contrasts, often with strong ecological and social underpinnings. As in earlier periods, art reflects a changing society and the issues and anxieties of the times. In paintings, sculpture, photographs, and installations, artists have either escaped into the beauty of the natural landscape or critically portrayed excessive consumerism and destruction of the environment while others have explored themes inspired by African mythology, blues and jazz, human folly, hard-edged inner city street life, Mardi Gras, pop culture, sexuality, spirituality, and the rhythms of breezes rising from the Mississippi River. In the late 1970s and 1980s, for instance, a small group of these artists, dubbed "Visionary Imagists" by art critic D. Eric Bookhardt, created colorful figurative images depicting ecological and spiritual concerns masked in what former CAC curator Lew Thomas called "audacious humor." Out in the streets, Orleans Parish Sheriff Charles Foti used art in the 1980s and 1990s to rehabilitate prisoners by having them paint bright murals on building walls and overpasses across the city. In addition, self-taught, or "outsider," artists such as Sister Gertrude Morgan received proper recognition, thanks to NOMA's 1993 show *Passionate Visions*, and women emerged as major forces not only as artists and gallery owners but also as museum curators and directors.

Photography also gained greater recognition and support. Photographers have produced a rich visual history of the city since 1840 with the first daguerreotypes by Jules Lion. Later in the century came city and rural landscapes by Samuel T. Blessing, Theodore Lilienthal, George Francois Mugnier, and Morgan Whitney. Federal Farm Security Administration photographers such as Walker Evans also left a lasting glimpse of Depression-era New Orleans. By the mid-twentieth century, photography as a fine art was expressed in the surrealism of Clarence John Laughlin and the moody and romantic

Located in the Arts (Warehouse) District, the Ogden Museum of Southern Art holds a comprehensive collection of Southern art and is noted for its original exhibitions, public events, and educational programs. (Courtesy of the Ogden Museum of Southern Art)

Sister Gertrude Morgan at the New Orleans Jazz & Heritage Festival   *Michael P. Smith, 1975*

Sister Gertrude Morgan (1900-1980) was born in Alabama. She was a self-taught poet, preacher, and critically acclaimed artist. For many years, Morgan sold her paintings at the New Orleans Jazz and Heritage Festival. (Photo by Michael P. Smith, 1975. Courtesy of The Historic New Orleans Collection.)

images of Arnold Genthe, Joseph Woodson "Pops" Whitesell, and others. In more recent years, prolific photographers have continued to gain regional and national acclaim as they explore the region's natural and cultural landscape.

With vernacular voices of their own, New Orleans artists have always remained aware of national trends. But there was a difference, claimed gallery owner Denise Berthiaume in a 1999 interview: "New York art is more abstract. We have more soul." In an exhibit of Louisiana art that traveled to London in 1996, British art historian Edward Lucie-Smith got at the heart of New Orleans and South Louisiana art:

> Louisiana art appears to have a distinct character which makes it different from that produced in other parts of the South . . . For example, artists often make use of imagery, which reflects the annual festival of Mardi Gras. . . . African-American art [also] has a growing presence which is not always found in the southern cultural mix. . . . In the case of Louisiana this may well be a certain pervasive romanticism. . . . By living and working in New Orleans and the area immediately around it, artists offer themselves a certain liberty to reject the fads, which often sweep the New York art world.

Then on August 29, 2005, Hurricane Katrina slammed southeast Louisiana and the Mississippi Gulf Coast. Three centuries of history and a singular culture seemed destined to perish under floodwaters. New Orleans had become what Walker Percy once described as a "Catholic limbo somewhere between the outer circle of Hell . . . and the inner circle of Purgatory." In the months after the storm, art became a catharsis in the city's recovery. The Ogden and THNOC reopened in October, while the heavily damaged CAC remained closed until January and NOMA until March. To help artists rebound, the Getty Foundation gave almost $3 million to local cultural institutions, and, in 2008, the New York art world and local galleries staged *Prospect.1 New Orleans*, the first of four citywide contemporary art shows that drew artists and visitors from all over the world. Locally, art galleries were among the first businesses to reopen and gather artists who had scattered across the country. As politicians squabbled, artists worked through the ruins to absorb the destruction, despair, and uncontrollable events rushing before them. "Emotion is easier to capture in difficult times than in good times," explained Rolland Golden, reflecting upon his experiences while painting his Katrina series for a 2007 exhibition at NOMA. "It's like being a masochist and hurting yourself every day. We express our deepest souls during times like these." Ironically, the international post-Katrina publicity attracted young artists from across the nation who moved to the city and, with local artists, created a vibrant new art scene in the Bywater, Marigny, and St. Roch neighborhoods.

Home for Thanksgiving, *2006. Painting by Rolland Golden. In the months following Hurricane Katrina, scores of artists worked through the ruins across New Orleans to capture the destruction, despair, and anger.* (In the Collection of Sonya and Renaud Rodrigue)

*Like many artists of the late nineteenth and twentieth centuries, the Australian-born New Orleans artist Simon Gunning continues to find artistic inspiration in the natural landscape. (*Big Bend, *painting by Simon Gunning, courtesy of Arthur Roger Gallery)*

Though art has always been important in New Orleans, the city now has more art galleries and working artists than in any other time in its three-century history. And like generations before them, these artists continue to create visions of New Orleans where, as the late surrealist photographer Clarence John Laughlin once wrote, "symbols have a life of their own."

John R. Kemp has written, edited, and contributed chapters for seventeen books on Louisiana art and history, including New Orleans: An Illustrated History, Martin Behrman of New Orleans: Memoirs of a City Boss, Louisiana's Black Heritage *(coeditor),* The Uniting States: The Story of Statehood for the Fifty United States of America, Expressions of Place: The Contemporary Louisiana Landscape, *and* A Unique Slant of Light: The Bicentennial History of Art in Louisiana *(coeditor). He also writes about Southern artists for regional and national magazines, including* Louisiana Life *and the New York-based* ARTnews, *and covers New Orleans art for the WYES show* Steppin' Out.

Congo Square, later called Beauregard Square and now part of Armstrong Park, was a gathering place for slaves in the eighteenth and part of the nineteenth centuries. They were allowed to engage in dances and trade goods. It became a major tourist attraction for many years. (Courtesy of The Historic New Orleans Collection.)

SALE OF ESTATES, PICTURES AND SLAVES IN THE ROTUNDA, NEW ORLEANS.

The rotunda in the St. Louis Hotel on Royal Street was the setting for the sale of slaves in the 1800s through Emancipation. On the site today is the Omni Royal Orleans. (Courtesy of The Historic New Orleans Collection)

Reversing the Blackout

Raphael Cassimere

Ernest N. "Dutch" Morial's election to the House of Representatives in 1968 ended a seven-decade blackout of black representation in the legislature. This was a small step for New Orleans' sesquicentennial. It began a snail's-pace selection of other African American officeholders across the city. Ten years later, Morial became the city's first black mayor. His success was not inevitable. He was not a favored protégé mentored by progressive whites who wished to reward black citizens after they had "proved" themselves. Instead, his was one of many hard-fought victories by black Louisianians to regain full citizenship rights that their ancestors had won a century earlier when they helped to write Louisiana's first post-Civil War constitution.

That constitution provided full citizenship rights without regard to race or color. Unfortunately, racist opponents—bolstered by adverse judicial rulings, such as the *Plessy* decision, which sanctioned "separate but equal"—thwarted its implementation. Subsequently, gross inequities ensued for much of the next century.

Blacks were disappointed but did not despair; earlier generations had faced similar setbacks but learned survival and resilience in the face of tragedies, whether slavery, hurricanes, epidemics, or war. Adversity was a given in life, but achievements could be gained even amid adversity if one persevered and remained resilient. Regaining those lost rights became the continual goal for the next generations.

Located in the French Quarter, the St. Louis Hotel was considered one of the grandest hotels in the city. It lasted until Reconstruction. (Archival architectural drawings by Jim Blanchard)

Creole in a Red Headdress, *circa 1840. Antebellum New Orleans was a cosmopolitan city with a large population of free people of color active in all aspects of the city's commercial and cultural life. In 1840, approximately 41 percent of the city's population included free and enslaved African Americans. During that period, the term "Creole" meant native-born persons who were descendants of the city's colonial population. (Portrait by Jacques Guillaume Lucien Amans. Courtesy of The Historic New Orleans Collection.)*

Resilience allowed them to overcome "colored only" screens on the bus and "whites only" notices in public accommodations or in the job market. They learned protective methods against brutal police misconduct. Resilience sustained them after the local school board limited them to only six grades of education. They survived political disfranchisement, supported by the grandfather clause and white primaries.

For the first fifty years after the city's bicentennial, they fought to gain basic civil and political rights, and by 1968, they had won back the right to vote and ended at least most forms of visible segregation in public accommodations and the workplace. While public and private schools remained largely racially segregated, at least they were moving beyond token desegregation. During the second half of the city's third century, the black middle class expanded as more black students not only completed high school but college as well, a sharp contrast to the first half of the twentieth century when less than a third of the city's black populace completed high school. In the past, underpaid and overworked black teachers served as successful role models and also embodied resilience in the face of insurmountable obstacles. Those sacrifices began to pay off as black administrators gradually moved into top administrative positions during the 1980s.

White students began to leave the system in droves, and except for one or two magnet schools, almost all schools had black student populations that exceeded ninety percent. Additionally, many middle-class black parents began to enroll their children in private schools, especially after the state began to provide more support for non-public schools. Paradoxically, the takeover by black officials coincided with increased accountability through high-stakes testing that often showed negative results for many black schools.

Taxpayers, including members of the black middle class, refused to raise taxes to support what many considered a failed system. Indeed, some of the younger black leaders were educated in private schools and showed less support for public education. Eventually, a state takeover of most of the city's public schools resulted in a smaller school district with fewer than a dozen schools under its control. However, state control did not provide the desired results, and, also due to the devastation caused by Hurricane Katrina, most local public schools became quasi-public, operating under individual charters. In 2016, prodded by black leaders and increasingly aware that state control had not achieved the desired result, the state legislature authorized return of most charter schools to local control by the city's tricentennial.

Older civil rights leaders had entered into politics as an extension of participation in the civil rights movement. Dutch Morial had served as president of the local NAACP, Rep. Avery Alexander had also served with the NAACP, and Rep. Johnny Jackson Jr. was a former CORE (Congress of Racial Equality) member. After passage of the 1965 Voting Rights Act, the sharp increase in black voters resulted in the election of black legislators, city council and school board members, tax assessors, clerks of court, sheriffs, and judges. Today, black judges serve at every level of the state judiciary, including the chief justice, Bernette J. Johnson.

Electoral success resulted in the rise of blacks into the upper levels of the city's civil service as well as membership on "blue ribbon" bodies such as the Board of Liquidation, City Debt and Armstrong Park and City Park commissions. Such members do not receive compensation but control huge sums of money by hiring bond attorneys and other highly paid financial consultants. Prior to Morial's mayoralty, none of these bodies had black members.

Morial served two terms and was followed in succession by three black mayors who each also served two terms: Sidney J. Barthelemy, Marc H. Morial, and C. Ray Nagin. Each faced a smaller population than his predecessor as white flight outdistanced the influx of new residents. The black mayor was never the traditional boss his white predecessors had been. The latter had more patronage to dispense prior to passage of "reform" laws that placed more appointive offices outside the control of the mayor. Additionally, taxpayers, including middle-class blacks, resisted much-needed tax increases to pay for crucial city services.

Early black officials learned how to win elections by forming coalitions based on racial solidarity, but they also had to learn to govern. The almost unanimity with which black voters supported their own candidates was a legacy of racial survival and resilience over the past centuries. On the other hand, black supporters had to learn to hold their own leaders accountable for adverse, illegal, or unethical actions. Black police chiefs, black district attorneys, and black judges did not lessen citizen complaints of police misconduct or a lack of basic services, contrary to promises black candidates made. Eventually, the conviction and removal of a number of black political officeholders increased cynicism among many and weakened their enthusiasm for black candidates. Therefore, in 2010 the thirty-two-year reign of black mayors ended with the election of a white candidate, Mitch Landrieu, who in 2014 was reelected with huge black support.

Black solidarity, on the other hand, increased in churches across denominational lines, albeit mostly in style rather than doctrine. Gospel music became the common thread. Black Christians were increasingly attracted to the Full Gospel movement, which infused traditional Protestant worship with high church features such as bishops dressed in more formal attire. Paul Morton, a Pentecostal transplant from Canada, founded the Full Gospel Baptist Church Fellowship and became its founding bishop. He combined elements of Pentecostalism with the black Baptist tradition while at the same time adding high church elements such as colorful clerical vestments and an episcopate—unknown and generally opposed by most Baptists—and, even more controversially, ordination of women into the ministry.

Today, black Catholic masses more closely resemble Protestant services than their white Catholic counterparts. Most black parishes have mass gospel choirs, and their parishioners clap and raise their hands in praise and shout "hallelujah!" and "amen!" At his consecration, Fernand J. Cheri, Auxiliary Bishop of New Orleans, gave his "testimony," a tradition unknown to most Catholics but familiar to Baptists and Pentecostals. When Cheri broke into song, he was joined by black parishioners while most whites in the cathedral looked on with bemused silence. Recently, one Catholic parish held a tent meeting revival in a public park. While most older black Catholics and Protestants rarely attended the other's church, today many worship together with little hesitation.

Because of a common history of economic inequities, black New Orleanians learned how to have a good time by working together and sharing. Whoever coined the term *laissez les bons temps rouler* must have had black New Orleanians in mind. Outsiders are always fascinated by poor or working-class people who live carefree lives amid myriad social problems. But despite internal and external hardships, they learned to live well, especially to eat "on the cheap."

They learned from their ancestors how to cook inexpensive but delectable dishes. Whether uptown or downtown, most cooked red beans and rice on Mondays. Some black restaurants began in the family home and expanded into small neighborhood restaurants. They served inexpensive, hearty breakfasts and

Dooky Chase's Restaurant, founded in 1941, is located in the Tremé neighborhood. It was considered a mecca by black New Orleanians before the passage of the Civil Rights Bill and a gathering place for early civil rights activism. Numerous famous music stars, such as Dizzy Gillespie and Charlie Parker, have been patrons, as have presidents, including Barack Obama. Today this beloved restaurant attracts diners not only locally but from around the world. (Photo by Peggy Scott Laborde)

lunch. For many years, Orleans/Basin, Claiborne, and St. Bernard Avenues were dotted with small neighborhood restaurants that served cheap Creole fare. Uptowners found similar fare on Dryades Street. They were unpretentious and served food on paper or plastic plates with plastic utensils. Except for Dooky Chase's Restaurant, favored by downtowners, or Hayes Chicken Shack uptown, most did not serve food on linen tablecloths and chinaware. Sadly, few of these restaurants survived Katrina.

Black folks know how to put on a good party. Their celebrations are as elaborate as they are frequent: births, christenings, weddings, funerals, and sporting events—but especially Carnival. While such celebrations are almost as old as the city, they have changed over time, particularly over the past half century. For many years, blacks celebrated the Carnival season from Thanksgiving to Mardi Gras. To the uninformed outsider, it appears that they spend too much time having a good time. In actuality, they have "fun earning funds." Seamstresses, tailors, caterers, florists, musicians, and bands earn extra money, sometimes off the book, during Carnival.

For many years, blacks from across the city congregated in Tremé, the nation's oldest predominantly African American neighborhood. Makeshift stands where food and drink was sold were constructed along Claiborne Avenue from Canal Street to Esplanade Avenue. Revelers watched impromptu Mardi Gras Indian tribes parade behind "marching bands" of as few as two musicians, sometimes with homemade instruments. They were followed by second lines of black maids and porters dressed gaudily like movie stars or baby dolls. But that Tremé no longer exists.

For more than a century, black New Orleanians have "masked Indian," walking through the city's streets dressed in feathers and beads, shouting chants, and rattling tambourines. Their suits are hand-sewn and feature intricate beadwork and feathered headdresses in tribute to Native American and African ancestors. The costumes usually take up to a year to create. (Photo by Judi Bottoni)

The tradition of Mardi Gras Indians is passed down from one generation to another. (Photo by Judi Bottoni)

The Zulu parade has been a part of the New Orleans Carnival since the early 1900s. (Photo by Judi Bottoni)

Women also dress as Mardi Gras Indians and are known as Queens. (Photo by Judi Bottoni)

During the mid-1960s, an extension of Interstate 10 ripped through the heart of Tremé and displaced hundreds of black residents and dozens of black businesses. The oak tree-lined promenade that stretched along Claiborne was replaced with concrete pillars. Many black revelers still look back nostalgically for those good old days. Despite those challenges, black citizens learned to adjust to change, but the *joie de vivre* that always characterized black New Orleans was seriously, nearly fatally, challenged when Hurricane Katrina came to town in 2005.

No stranger to hurricanes, many longtime residents always rode out the storm at home. This time was different; those who failed to evacuate watched with horror as the city drowned around them. Others who escaped were equally traumatized as television portrayed the extent of the emergency. Many older residents were transported to distant places with names they could hardly pronounce.

Most evacuees were accepted warmly by their hosts in these strange places but suffered culture shock, bereft of their Creole fare. Those who remained or returned were shocked by the extent of the devastation. However, before too long, with the same resilience that had sustained their forbearers for nearly three centuries, they began to rebuild but also realized the city would probably never be the same again. They hoped they could help rebuild it better. Those who could not return made themselves feel at home by importing Camellia beans, chaurice sausage, dried shrimp, and crab boil, as well as visiting sports bars where they could watch their beloved Saints. Many died outside the city but were returned home for burial in their beloved N'awlins.

Following Katrina, many insisted New Orleans could not—perhaps should not—be rebuilt. However, returnees insisted that the city's burial plans were premature and its jazz funeral should be cancelled. New Orleans, they insisted, would be around not just for the moment but also long after its quadricentennial in 2118.

Dr. Raphael Cassimere Jr., a sixth-generation New Orleanian and a product of its public schools, earned his BA and MA degrees in history from UNO and his PhD from Lehigh University. He taught at UNO for thirty-seven years and retired as Seraphia D. Leyda Professor-Emeritus in 2007. He has been active with the NAACP and is past chair of the Vieux Carré Commission. Cassimere is the author of African Americans in New Orleans Before the Civil War *and numerous scholarly articles.*

Hotels and office buildings dot the downtown New Orleans skyline. (Photo by George Long)

The Times—Bad, Good, and Amazing

Peter Ricchiuti

For the last century or so, the New Orleans economy has been a three-legged stool held up by tourism, oil, and the port. While these are still vital, new industries and a surge of entrepreneurship have changed our economy, once slow, genteel, and tied tightly to location. Traditionally, big swings in commodity prices have sent the region through a series of booms and busts. The oil and gas industry has been truly mercurial. But with a more diversified and welcoming economy and a wave of talented newcomers post-Katrina, New Orleans has become one of the nation's brightest business prospects—without sacrificing our special way of life.

Oil and Gas

After World War II, the New Orleans area became the chief beneficiary of the advent of offshore drilling for oil and natural gas. The hunt for hydrocarbons had been going on here for a long while, but the ability to drill in the water is credited to Alden "Doc" Laborde. Laborde was a true business genius who started three publicly traded companies: ODECO (now a part of Diamond Offshore), New Orleans-based Tidewater, and Houma's Gulf Island Fabrication. There is a terrific movie called *Thunder Bay* about Doc Laborde and his invention of an industry. (Jimmy Stewart plays Doc Laborde. Come on—that's pretty cool!)

Laborde pitched his offshore drilling ideas to several oil companies before Murphy Oil joined forces on his offshore vision. The first offshore well (drilled out of sight of land) in the Gulf of Mexico was drilled by Kerr-McGee in 1947 in just forty feet of water. Suddenly, dock workers

Alden "Doc" Laborde is considered the father of offshore oil drilling in the Gulf of Mexico. (Courtesy of Jack Laborde)

The "Mr. Charlie" was the first transportable submersive oil rig. It was completed in 1953 and drilled hundreds of offshore wells. (Photo courtesy of Jack Laborde)

became roughnecks, shrimp trawlers were converted into offshore oilfield vessels, and the race was on. If you're a fan of oil patch nostalgia, the very first offshore rig, the Mr. Charlie (named after Charlie Murphy) is still available for tours over in Morgan City.

In 1960, five oil-producing nations banded together to found OPEC, the Organization of the Petroleum-Exporting Countries, aiming to control world oil markets. The move drove oil prices sky-high. It was a fiscal disaster for most of the nation but a boon to New Orleans. (Bumper stickers reading "Drive 70 and freeze a Yankee" didn't help this animosity.) Oil-drilling activity and necessary services such as rigs, boats, personnel, and offshore catering soared. New Orleans was a big player in energy. Poydras Street, our Central Business District, became a collection of impressive office towers, and the names on these buildings told you where the city's bread was buttered: Amoco, Shell, Texaco, Tidewater.

All of this came to a screeching halt in the mid-1980s. OPEC set out to punish OPEC members who failed to abide by production quotas. The cartel flooded the market with oil and drove down oil prices. This put New Orleans and the area into a painful recession that lasted for several years.

The oil industry recovered slowly, and by the mid-1990s technology (and guts) enabled drillers to try their hand off the continental shelf. These deep-water offshore finds are impressive and now account for about eighty percent of all the oil produced from the Gulf of Mexico.

The deepest well to date was drilled in about 7,500 feet of water and another 29,000 feet beneath the seabed. That's 36,500 feet from the bottom of the derrick, or approximately seven miles. To put this in perspective, that's about how high a commercial jet flies on a transcontinental flight.

It was once explained to me that this kind of high-risk deep-water drilling was akin to "flying above New York City and trying to hit the pitcher's mound at

Yankee Stadium with a tool the size of a coffee can, at $10 billion a pop, in the dark." The technology is indeed impressive, and much of it was developed right here in Louisiana.

Then a massive explosion aboard BP's Deepwater Horizon rig in 2010 resulted in eleven deaths and the nation's biggest environmental disaster, spewing an estimated 4.9 million barrels of oil into the Gulf of Mexico. This taught the world about the risks of such deep-water projects and resulted in a controversial government moratorium on deep-water drilling.

In reaction to the prolific increase in US oil production, Saudi Arabia acted to protect its declining oil market share by increasing production and dramatically lowering oil prices. That resulted in another big contraction in oilfield jobs and projects, and in industry parlance the Gulf of Mexico has again become known as the Dead Sea.

However, it's important to note that since the 1980s, most of the big oil companies have consolidated their operations in Houston. As a result, these days the New Orleans economy is much more diversified and less affected by the oil industry's ups and downs.

Transportation and the Port

Talk about a strategic location. The Port of New Orleans is the busiest waterway in the world and the only US seaport to be served by all six major railroads: CSX, Norfolk Southern, BNSF, Canadian National, Union Pacific, and Kansas City Southern.

Each year more than 11,000 vessels traverse the lower Mississippi River, hauling diverse items such as rubber, plywood, and poultry. More than 160,000 jobs are connected to the port and its operations. Competition with Miami, Houston, and other ports along the Gulf Coast is fierce, and since World War II, the Port of New Orleans has spent billions upgrading and modernizing its facilities.

The Louisiana Offshore Oil Platform, an engineering marvel completed in 1972, allows huge oil tankers too big to navigate the Mississippi River to offload their cargo into underwater salt domes, where it awaits transport by pipeline to the nation's refineries.

In 1993 the port scored a major victory in landing the Silocaf project, the world's biggest bulk coffee handling plant.

Meanwhile, container transport makes up an ever-larger share of the shipping market. In 2004, the port upgraded and moved its primary container facilities uptown to its Napoleon Avenue terminal.

New Orleans has entered the cruise ship business in a big way. In 2006, the Erato Street Cruise Terminal and parking garage were opened. This growing business has supplied an extra ripple effect to the city's economy as cruise-goers routinely tack on a few extra days before and after their cruise to enjoy New Orleans.

Not all attempts at accelerating commerce have worked out for the better. In 1965 the Army Corps of Engineers completed the Mississippi River-Gulf Outlet, or the MRGO. This passageway, often referred to as "the Mr. Go," was a kind of shortcut allowing ever-larger vessels to avoid the twists and turns of the river by utilizing the Intracoastal Waterway. But the Mr. Go never attracted as much traffic as was predicted. It created numerous environmental problems (particularly erosion) and inadvertently became a "hurricane highway," which is blamed for worsening the flooding from Hurricane Katrina in 2005. The damage done, the Mr. Go has now been permanently closed.

As a transportation hub, New Orleans is still affected by trade policies and shifts in the world economy, but the widening of the Panama Canal and warming relations with Cuba could be huge plusses down the road.

Tourism

Tourism has always been a staple of the New Orleans economy and has now become a juggernaut thanks to both leisure and business visitors. About ten million people visit the city each year, spending more than $7 billion while they're here.

A huge catalyst for the growth in tourism came in the form of the Ernest N. Morial Convention Center. Named after the city's former mayor, the ever-expanding facility sits just upriver from the French Quarter. Initial parts of the convention center were built in 1984 a part of the World's Fair. The Fair itself was an economic disaster, but it sparked the development not only of the convention center but also of the city's vibrant Warehouse District. The World's Fair is still remembered fondly by locals and featured a lovable "spokes-pelican" named Seymour D. Fair (best mascot name ever.)

The development of the Convention Center put New Orleans in the running for large conferences, and the city is now one of the top hosts of business meetings and conventions in the nation.

The Louisiana Superdome was erected in 1971 (and, of course, remodeled after Hurricane Katrina) and holds about 76,500 fans. Now the Mercedes-Benz Superdome, it is not only the home of the NFL's New Orleans Saints and a recognizable icon on the skyline but also a powerful asset in attracting conventions and major events to the city. The Smoothie King Center right next door, with a capacity of 18,000, is the home of the NBA's New Orleans Pelicans. In combination with the convention center, the two stadiums open up a world of opportunities for big-meeting planners.

All of this has ushered in a new level of growth in visitors. New Orleans has become such an attractive destination that tourism officials are luring travelers to expand their horizons beyond traditional (often crowded) areas such as the French Quarter and into the city's other interesting neighborhoods.

The tourism appeal of New Orleans continues to grow. In addition to Mardi Gras (an economic shot in the arm worth more than $450 million annually), other yearly events such as the New Orleans Jazz and Heritage Festival, Voodoo Festival, sporting events, and myriad food-related extravaganzas keep the city hopping. The summer is hot and sticky and, in the past, was a slow time in New Orleans. But now, thanks to big events such as the Essence Festival in July and Satchmo Summerfest in August, even the summers are bustling.

The New Orleans airport (now named after local jazz hero Louis Armstrong) helps transport these throngs into our region, but it is often criticized as too small and lacking many nonstop flights. Site selection gurus argue that a high-quality airport is the single biggest determinant for a company's location decisions. With this in mind, plans for a brand-new airport (next to the existing facility) were unveiled. This new facility is expected to boost tourism, cargo, and business travel.

Frankly, nobody can put on a party like New Orleans. (Have you ever run into anyone hoping and praying for another Super Bowl in Minneapolis or

Cincinnati?) To the visitor, all of this seems like fun and games—as it should. But to the nearly 90,000 people employed in tourism, it's a job and a seriously big business.

New Ideas, New Industries, New Jobs

The city has never been a corporate mecca. In fact, there is only one Fortune 500 company, Entergy, in New Orleans. Attracting these companies has always been a hard sell. Even companies that originated here changed ownership and moved their headquarters when they reached a certain size—Popeyes to Atlanta, for example, and Ruth's Chris Steak House to Orlando. Other successful brands such as spice-maker Zatarain's and Barq's root beer have been swallowed up by bigger players in their industries.

In the past, crime and poor education (not unrelated) kept businesses from even considering moving their jobs to the Crescent City, particularly white-collar ones. While our relatively low cost of living might have seemed a valuable lure in attracting business, corporate leaders felt that public schools were generally not an option for their employees. After adding in private school tuition, the area wasn't really such a bargain.

A parochial, close-knit business community was, until Hurricane Katrina, not all that welcoming to newcomers. These days it's a meritocracy with lots of enthusiastic and well-educated young people moving into town. New Orleans has been named the "Coolest Start-Up City in America" by *Inc. Magazine,* and the *Wall Street Journal* congratulated New Orleans on having "the most improved economy in the USA." Smart, innovative, technology-driven businesses are dotting the landscape.

The city's first business accelerator was the Idea Village, which opened in 2000. There are now several incubators here, and each spring New Orleans Entrepreneur Week showcases the best and most interesting business ideas. The rise of the area's social entrepreneurship community is particularly promising. Here, folks apply innovative business techniques to solve societal problems, of which there is no shortage.

This may sound a bit more mundane, but for decades New Orleanians in need of clothes and other day-to-day goods often traveled to neighboring Jefferson Parish for their shopping. Post-Katrina has seen a slew of new retail outlets within the city limits. In his first inauguration, Mayor Mitch Landrieu said that he "wanted the mayor of New Orleans to be able to buy underwear in his own parish" (this got a lot of applause). New retail sales taxes have raised, and made more predictable, the city's revenue stream and helped lead to a bond rating increase.

But by some metrics, New Orleans has fallen mightily since World War II. The city had a peak population of more than 600,000 back in 1960. When Katrina hit, the population had dropped to just 500,000 residents, and today it has only about 350,000. Measured another way, thirty years ago we were the thirty-fourth-largest media market, and we have fallen to the fifty-first.

Holding Business Back

A legacy of crooked politics made doing business in the area a nightmare. The city's former mayor, Ray Nagin, Congressman William Jefferson, and Jefferson Parish President Aaron Broussard have all been sent to the pokey.

Coastal erosion and the area's vulnerability to storms have also made business leaders think twice about settling down here. We're losing about a football field of land each hour. (As comedian Stephen Colbert remarked, "Pretty soon those people won't have any place to play football!")

Post-Katrina New Orleans has been called the "Greatest Comeback Since Lazarus." In particular, the business climate has improved since the storm.

Business is now much more welcoming to outsiders who have flocked to the city for work. Traditional schools have been replaced with charter schools. We now have more idealistic young Teach for America educators than any other city, and New Orleans has become America's petri dish for innovation in education. Many of the city's new innovators and entrepreneurs have focused on education-related products.

Increased community involvement in local government is leading to growing accountability for our politicians. Political structures themselves are changing. Before the storm, the city elected seven separate tax assessors and property valuations were uneven (to put it kindly). Now there is a single assessor and assessed home values are available publicly online.

Large numbers of people have moved into New Orleans. They tend to be young, well educated, and in love with New Orleans. Population booms in the past, particularly in the oilfield, may have brought residents here "against their will," a kind of sentence to serve as they moved up in their careers. Many of these people avoided time in New Orleans and opted to live on the other side of Lake Pontchartrain. This migration feels very different.

These newcomers are living uptown, in the Garden District, in Mid-City, downtown, in the Marigny and Bywater. The best example of the change in the business environment is actually in the city's Central Business District. Until about twenty years ago, the CBD was made up of several office towers, the Superdome, and a series of sad, neglected older buildings and surface parking lots. This unappealing visual effect is referred to in architectural circles as a "jack-o'-lantern" cityscape. Now new and renovated apartments, restaurants, condominiums, retail spaces, entertainment venues, and the mammoth University Medical Center have increased downtown's density. No longer deserted after dark, the CBD is a place to be seen at all hours.

Not every new development in commerce has had legs. In 2002 the Louisiana State Legislature created a tax credit program to attract moviemakers and digital designers to the state. By 2014, more movies were being made in New Orleans than in any city in the nation. Jobs grew by leaps and bounds, and celebrities were sighted standing in line at grocery stores or biking through the Quarter. In 2016, massive state budget deficits and scandals regarding the tax credits themselves caused cutbacks in the tax breaks, made the state less attractive to the industry, and sent actors, clapboards, and production trucks off into the sunset.

Yes, for a while hurricanes and environmental disasters made doing business in New Orleans feel a bit like living in Old Testament times. But this city is nothing if not resilient. We love our local business institutions, and no city has done a better job of holding back the soul-destroying homogenization that is modern America. The holy grail here is to grow the economy without losing what makes New Orleans so special.

Peter Ricchiuti teaches finance at Tulane University's A. B. Freeman School of Business and hosts a weekly business show on the local national public radio affiliate WWNO in New Orleans. He is the author of the investment book Stocks Under Rocks: How to Uncover Overlooked, Profitable Market Opportunities.

Evolution of a Festive Town

Errol Laborde

At approximately nine o'clock in the evening on Tuesday, February 24, 1857, the art of celebrating in New Orleans was born. There had been revelry, rowdiness, and grandeur in the town, which by that year was already 139 years old, but nothing with any lasting style and direction. Because the town was largely Catholic, the Christian holidays were celebrated; because of its French origin, there was deference to the tradition of Mardi Gras, preceding Lent, but really nothing special.

That changed, though, on that evening in 1857. Few cities in the world can claim a specific style of celebration, but that is what began on that winter night.

From the vicinity of the corner of Camp and Julia Streets came a parade unlike anything ever seen. Masked men marched in a procession that included floats, decorated to glitter with the light of the accompanying torches, gently rocking to the lay of the street, and carrying none other than Satan himself: "The glare of torchlights shattered the darkness . . . bands burst into symphony, and the Mistick Krewe stood revealed—a company of demons, rich and realistic, moving in a procession that seemed to blaze from some secret chamber of the earth," historian Perry Young would write of that moment. In his 1931 classic, *The Mistick Krewe: Chronicles of Comus and His Kin*, Young told of Comus having borrowed its spirit and costumes from Mobile's raucous Cowbellians. The fanciful group proceeded up Julia Street to St. Charles, turning right past the seat of government, Gallier Hall. The parade itself was a stage, though one that moved past the waiting audience. On that night, Mardi Gras would become more than just an entry on the French calendar but an institution that would be defined for North America by New Orleans and would shape practically all other celebrations to come.

With Comus having flipped the switch, seemingly each following year would bring more to the Carnival celebration. Beginning in 1870, the Twelfth Night Revelers started marching each January 6, the date being the opening of the Carnival season. With Comus parading in the season's final moments, the Revelers became the bookend at the beginning.

In 1872 Carnival achieved its biggest moment. In that year, the fifteenth since Comus first paraded, a new group named Rex, the Latin for "king," took to the street. Self-proclaimed but unchallenged as the king of Carnival, he introduced an important innovation, parading during the daylight hours. From then on, Carnival's celebration became more than an after-hours pastime.

With the celebration focused on a Tuesday afternoon, organizers faced a decision: either become responsible for high workplace absenteeism, or make Mardi Gras a holiday. The choice was easy. Once that happened, the New Orleans celebration could grow, not only among locals but also by attracting visitors. In 1872, people didn't talk about "economic development," but by having a parade that was good enough in a setting popular enough, that could happen. The need to be loved was especially acute because the city, like many other Southern towns at the time, was trying to re-enter the mainstream of the American economy that had been left staggering by the Civil War. Carnival was not only a means of celebrating but also a source of financial growth, a truth that made it easier for city leaders to justify the supporting expenses.

Like the concentric ripples in a stream once a stone is tossed into it, the Carnival celebration would grow mightily to eventually include parades practically every day over a two-week period, as well as Carnival balls, bigger and glitzier processions, packed hotel rooms, and new industries, one of the most gluten-glorious being the baking of king cakes.

Through the next two centuries, Carnival would develop its own menagerie of characters and krewes, some unique and exclusive in their own way but the totality being mixed in size, gender, and race. The black community made its participation known with the establishment of the Zulu parade in 1909, which originally gently

An 1850 Harpers' Weekly *depiction of the second Mistick Krewe of Comus parade.*

To improve the local economy after Reconstruction, a group of citizens created Rex, New Orleans' first daytime parade, as a way of attracting visitors. (Painting by George Schmidt)

Riding past Gallier Hall on the city's most historic mode of transportation, the historic Phunny Phorty Phellows carnival organization kicks off the Carnival season on Twelfth Night. (Photo by Judi Bottoni)

poked fun at the white Mardi Gras while winding its way through black neighborhoods.

Carnival set the image of New Orleans as a fun and desirable place to be, so much so that the satirist Ring Lardner once wrote of his Carnival experience that by Ash Wednesday he felt like "Rex in the state of Comus."

From New Orleans emerged the model for what would become the American-style Mardi Gras. Other places borrowed bits and pieces of the city's Carnival, including purple, green, and gold as colors; the language, especially the use of the word "krewe" (a Comus invention); and usually shabbier versions of parades with maskers flinging beads and doubloons from decorated truck beds. Even Mobile, which provided some of the earlier influences for establishing Comus, changed into a New Orleans-style Carnival.

Carnival's influence would also take an inward turn, providing a model for other celebrations not related to the season. The parade of the local Irish, on or near St. Patrick's Day, features riders in floats who toss cabbage and trinkets Carnival style. A Halloween parade borrowed from Carnival to call itself the Krewe of Boo. Within the black community evolved one of Carnival's richest, and purest, customs: the Mardi Gras Indians, wearing rich, feathery costumes far more glamorous than what was worn by native tribes. The Indians once performed exclusively on Mardi Gras but extended their celebration to a weekend near St. Joseph's Day.

Eventually, the Indians would bridge Carnival and another event that would

Members of the Society of St. Cecilia, who wear creative and often very colorful costumes on Mardi Gras Day. (Photo by Peggy Scott Laborde)

A Mardi Gras Indian at the corner of North Claiborne and Orleans avenues, a traditional meeting point for various tribe members. (Photo by Armand "Sheik" Richardson)

Members of the Society of St. Anne walking club on Mardi Gras Day. (Photo by Peggy Scott Laborde)

Mardi Gras Day behind St. Louis Cathedral. (Photo by Peggy Scott Laborde)

The opening-day parade of French Quarter Festival. (Photo by George Long)

become the second force in developing the city's celebration profile. Begun in 1970 and first held in Congo Square at Armstrong Park, the New Orleans Jazz and Heritage Festival (more commonly known as Jazz Fest) moved to the Fair Grounds racetrack in 1972. There it belongs and should always stay. The gated complex with its lush infield and spacious grandstand area is perfect for the event.

There are music festivals throughout the world; Jazz Fest is arguably among the top echelon. (Actually there is no argument; it is the very best.) Two things set it apart: the variety of music, which is considerably more than jazz, and the quality of foods and crafts. Music groups are not alone in having to prove themselves worthy of being there; so too do food vendors and artists. Just as the Jazz Fest has given bands exposure (one year including a startling combination of the Preservation Hall Jazz Band and Del McCoury's bluegrass group, both representing Southern music art forms), so too do locals now relish *cochon de lait* po' boys (made with the tender meat of a young pig) and Crawfish Monica, a creamy pasta. Despite the casual look of the festival and its sandal-clad celebrants, everything there is done well and with efficiency. Unlike the experience at many music clubs, acts at the Fest begin and end on time.

The Mardi Gras Indians' annual path now includes not just the backstreets on Mardi Gras morning but also the infield of the fairgrounds. Borrowing from the clothing of the Plains Indians and dancing to their own spin of Afro-Caribbean music, the Indians are a totally indigenous custom born of New Orleans' black community but influenced by the cultural milieu of a port city. No place else could have such a heritage mix.

Besides giving the Indians a chance to be seen by more people than the number who would spot them along their circuitous Mardi Gras morning path, Jazz Fest has given other performers—most notably gospel groups as well as Cajun and zydeco purveyors—reason to continue to be. By its influence, the Fest has had a trickle-down effect around town through the year, including the French Quarter Fest and the Voodoo Fest, both outdoor musical events where the beat continues.

Look at practically any event in this city filled with festivals and there is the influence of Mardi Gras, Jazz Fest, or both.

Yet there are key differences between these two celebrations that give each its own individuality: Jazz Fest charges admission; Mardi Gras calls itself the greatest free show on earth. Jazz Fest has commercial sponsors; sponsorship is not allowed in New Orleans' Carnival parades. Jazz Fest is run by a private nonprofit organization; Mardi Gras is like a parade with many different moving parts working, somewhat miraculously, as a confederation. Jazz Fest is gated; Mardi Gras is not. Mardi Gras has a deep-rooted social element among some of its krewes; for the Jazz Fest, the musicians are the royalty.

Many towns have festivals and various causes to celebrate. New Orleans just seems to have more and to be better at it for several reasons, including a semi-tropical climate that is cooperative most of the year; a strong tourist base that attracts festival-goers and that in turn generates more festivals; and, not to be overlooked, great settings. Among those are the French Quarter, the riverfront, Lafayette Square, City Park, Audubon Park, and of course the Fair Grounds. The settings alone are rich for whimsy. For example, the annual Tennessee Williams/New Orleans Literary Festival is global in quality, bringing in top scholars, authors, and performers. It is, as a festival-goer once commented, a "feast for the mind." Yet its founders discovered the need for a visual jolt, and thus was created the annual Stanley and Stella shouting contest. On the closing Sunday of each festival, a crowd gathers at Jackson Square to hear contestants parody Stanley Kowalski's yell of "Stella!" from Williams' *A Streetcar Named Desire*—or, in deference to the time, a cry of "Stanley!" (Judges stationed on a Pontalba building balcony assess the yells from below, not unlike float-riders, though awarding points rather than trinkets.) The event has gotten international attention, partially through the miracle of YouTube. Surprisingly, what was created to be a publicity gimmick has proved to have educational value as more people have wondered about Stanley, Stella, and what the shouting is all about.

Then there are situations when the proper response is not shouting but polite applause. At approximately 11:30 each Mardi Gras evening, Comus, the god whose parade started it all back in 1857, greets Rex, King of Carnival, and his consort, the Queen of Carnival. In what is the most scripted ritual of all the city's celebrations, the monarchs bow to each other and then promenade around the ballroom floor to the stirring music of *Aida*'s "Grand March."

This ceremony, known as the Meeting of the Courts, has been Carnival's final act every Mardi Gras night since 1882. It is televised to a large audience, many of whom through the years have come to know each nuance and movement by heart.

After a period of general dancing, the Comus captain will ceremoniously

The Meeting of the Courts of Rex and the Mistick Krewe of Comus marks the end of the Carnival Season. (Photo by Estelle deVerges)

escort each of the monarchs out of the ballroom and then lead his lieutenants to a spot on the floor where the last vision of Carnival will be the curtain closing. In no other city in the world is the closing ritual of a celebration included in a television listing. As Comus the Greek god for a day heads toward his changing room to morph back into a private citizen, Comus the myth prevails: with the curtain closed, the party is over; the clock moves toward Lent.

Ash Wednesday's solemnity is respected more in New Orleans than in most cities, partially because Carnival's unbridled spirit of feasting before fasting has made the fasting that follows more welcome, if only for a day. On Ash Wednesday, it is common to see locals returning to the office with a black smudge on their foreheads, the remains of an ashen cross thumb-painted by a priest to remind them of "dust to dust." Ash Wednesday is a welcomed day for cleansing, not just the soul but also the streets. Yet its sober message cannot linger. With the celebrations of St. Patrick and St. Joseph only a few weeks away, there will be serious feasting to be done. The celebrating begins anew.

In thanks for favors granted, the ancient Sicilian tradition of creating St. Joseph Altars is celebrated by creating an altar of Lenten foodstuffs. This one is located at St. Joseph Catholic Church on Tulane Avenue. (Photo by Peggy Scott Laborde)

Tiles with "Thanks" inscribed on them are inserted on the floor of an alcove within the tiny chapel in St. Roch Cemetery. (Photo by Peggy Scott Laborde)

Errol Laborde is the Executive Vice President and Editor in Chief of Renaissance Publishing Company. The winner of over twenty New Orleans Press Club awards, Laborde is a three-time winner of the Alex Waller Award, the highest award given in print journalism by the Press Club. He received the Press Club's Lifetime Achievement award in 2016. In 2013, Laborde won a national award from the City and Regional Magazine Association when he took first place in the column writing category. Laborde holds a PhD in political science from the University of New Orleans.

Times of Obsession

Angus Lind

Country singer and songwriter Jerry Jeff Walker—no stranger to New Orleans—released "It Don't Matter" in 2001. The pertinent lyrics are:

Down in Louisiana, it don't matter
If you're sane as a judge or mad as a hatter.

And it's been that way ever since the Frenchman Bienville founded New Orleans in 1718—except that several of our jurists have strayed from sanity.

"New Orleans has always been a risky business," wrote New Orleans historian Mel Leavitt in his 1984 book, *Great Characters of New Orleans*. "It naturally attracted dreamers and schemers, soldiers of fortune, gamblers, fanatics, people who had reached land's (or wit's) end—and those who merely hoped to start life over again."

Blame it on the French, but from the city's inception, there has been a *laissez les bons temps rouler* ("let the good times roll") and *joie de vivre* ("carefree enjoyment of life") mentality that pervades the city. Our priorities are different. Food, drink, music, and partying head the list. We worship leisure time.

Like swamps for mosquitoes, this laidback lifestyle provides the perfect breeding ground for characters. New Orleans is a safe haven where eccentrics, renegades, rogues, rounders, and rascals are not only tolerated but embraced and glorified. Ditto for make-believe kings and queens.

More often than not, the characters are not public figures. Instead, they operate in the shadows because many of them are or were gamblers, con artists, racetrackers, boxing promoters, bartenders, card sharks, hustlers, masters of obfuscation, wannabe politicos, even mobsters and crooks. Without a voice to publicize them, these shadowy figures would remain in the shadows. But with newsmen trumpeting their eccentricities, foibles, and personalities, they come to life and become characters known to the public.

Twentieth-century New York was once the domain of the legendary newsman Damon Runyon, who roamed the streets and brought to the forefront the likes of Nathan Detroit, Harry the Horse, and Big Jule. In New Orleans, the task fell to several newspaper columnists who frequented their hangouts. But to lay the groundwork for a sampling of some of the city's top characters of the past half century, you have to understand who some of the most celebrated and famous characters have been.

Josie Arlington was a bawdy, rich, and influential madam who from 1897 to 1917 ruled all of Storyville, the city's infamous and legal thirty-eight-block red light district centered on Basin Street, flush with dance halls, bars, and great jazz musicians. Josie and her prostitution empire were fully protected by the law. Then there was the brazen pirate Jean Lafitte. With his Baratarians, Lafitte plundered ships in the Caribbean and smuggled and sold stolen goods, only to be recruited by Gen. Andrew Jackson to help him defeat the British in the 1815 Battle of New Orleans—and forever be a folk hero. Throw in Marie Laveau, the Voodoo Queen whose *gris gris*, black magic, and potions were widely revered in the nineteenth century. She held public voodoo rituals on Bayou St. John where she beheaded live roosters and drank their blood. And then there was Bernard de Marigny, an incorrigible nineteenth-century gambler and playboy who squandered millions, introduced the dice game craps to America, and was responsible for the naming of streets such as Good Children, Desire, Elysian Fields, and Craps in his failed attempt to develop Faubourg Marigny—and you can see that more recent characters have a lot to live up to.

In the 1960s through the 1990s, this city had a thriving colony of hilarious eccentrics. Two guys set the bar very high: Allen "Black Cat" LaCombe and Rodney "Get the Gorilla" Fertel, who were compadres.

LaCombe, the legendary Fair Grounds handicapper and publicity director, ran for governor in 1959 on a dare from the bar rats at Curley's Neutral Corner, a sports bar at Poydras and St. Charles where racetrackers, boxing fans, and the media hung out—"da news guys," as LaCombe described them. Proprietor

Curley Gagliano was the proprietor of Curley's Neutral Corner, a sports bar at Poydras and St. Charles where gamblers, hustlers, boxing fans, and the media hung out. On a dare from the bar rats there, "Black Cat" LaCombe decided to run for governor in 1959 and Curley, who was bald, put up the $250 qualifying fee. LaCombe finished "up the track" in horseracing parlance. (Courtesy of Angus Lind)

Every year during his tenure at the Fair Grounds, LaCombe hosted a post-Kentucky Derby red beans and rice dinner for "da news guys." There was an earlier contest to pick the order of finish in the Derby. The winners got steak; the losers got red beans. Here LaCombe presents the Worst Handicapper Award to Angus Lind. (Courtesy of Angus Lind)

The uncrowned king of local characters, Fair Grounds Race Course handicapper and publicity director Allen "Black Cat" LaCombe was beloved by the media. (Courtesy of Angus Lind)

Curley Gagliano, who was bald, put up the $250 qualifying fee for the Black Cat to run against favored Jimmie Davis. His campaign slogan was "Run the squirrels out of office—keeps the state safe for the nuts." One night on the campaign trail in LaCombe's hometown of Echo in Avoyelles Parish, LaCombe told the gathered crowd to vote for Davis' rival, wealthy radio magnate Jimmy Noe, because a vote for LaCombe would be a wasted vote. Afterward, Noe greased LaCombe's palm with several $100 bills, and Black Cat made sure he always showed up wherever Noe was campaigning. LaCombe was no stranger to hustling.

As it turned out, Davis went around the state playing his guitar, singing "You Are My Sunshine," and won. LaCombe finished "up the track," in bettors' parlance—seventh in a field of nine.

LaCombe grew up in the Irish Channel and spoke with a heavy Y'at accent—"dese" and "dose" and "dem." After being drafted during World War II, he threw a party for his draft board. As handicapper for the old *States-Item* afternoon newspaper, he once picked nine straight winners—and didn't bet on one of them. "I got touted off," he explained. He wore one black sock and one brown sock for good luck, but it didn't work. He called everybody "cuz" and wore a black bowler he said had been blessed by the pope. He was, as late sports columnist Peter Finney observed, "a real beauty."

In 1965, he and clothier Joe Gemelli, another LaCombe sidekick, invited Johnny Carson, then host of NBC-TV's *The Tonight Show*, to come to devastated New Orleans for a Hurricane Betsy benefit, Gemelli telling Carson's agent he was Mayor Vic Schiro. When the agent said he would get back to the mayor quickly, the pair high-tailed it to the mayor's office. Schiro had to leave for appointments, so they slipped in and then fielded the telephone call and sealed the deal for Carson to visit. The con worked, the benefit was a huge success, and afterward they took Carson to Diamond Jim Moran's La Louisiane restaurant, where Carson chipped a tooth on one of Moran's patented meatballs with a diamond in it, causing him to miss his show the next night.

LaCombe had almost as many friends as he had losing tickets. In declining health in 1987, a group of "da news guys" threw a benefit for the Black Cat at the Fair Grounds to honor him. Tickets were $13 apiece. The crowd was enormous and predictably Runyonesque—someone even walked off with part of the gate. The Cat kept his antics going until 1989, ending his gig in a hearse that did a lap around the Fair Grounds oval as the track bugler played the "Call to the Post" followed by "Taps."

In 1969, Rodney Fertel, a gambler, racetracker, and world traveler who had inherited a fortune in CBD real estate and a successful pawnshop—and who at one time was married to Ruth Fertel, founder of the Ruth's Chris Steak House empire—ran for mayor. It was a campaign never before seen in this city or anywhere else. He pledged that if elected he would get a gorilla for the zoo. "Don't settle for a monkey," said the candidate. "Elect Fertel and get a gorilla. If elected, I will conduct a personal safari to the Belgian Congo at my own expense and bring back two live gorillas to the Audubon Zoo."

As difficult as this may be to believe, Fertel purchased thousands of miniature toy gorillas—half white and half black so that, in his mind, people would know he did not harbor any racial prejudice. With none other than LaCombe as his campaign manager, Fertel put on a gorilla costume and stood at a corner on Canal Street handing out black gorillas to black passersby and white ones to white people. He passed out campaign buttons with King Kong's face on them. If he wasn't in his gorilla suit, he wore a safari outfit and a pith helmet and carried binoculars. In the November election that year, of the 176,736 votes cast in the Democratic primary, the Gorilla Man got 310. According to his son Randy Fertel's 2011 book, *The Gorilla Man and the Empress of Steak*, on seeing the results, the Black Cat said, "I didn't know dey had dat many gorillas in New Oryuns."

So the next mayor was not Rodney Fertel but Moon Landrieu. And what did Fertel do? He kept his promise. In 1970 he flew to Singapore, which even the geographically impaired will tell you is nowhere near the Belgian Congo. He began his search for the gorillas, sending letters to two *States-Item* reporters informing them of his progress. Months went by, and the letters kept showing up. Then one day a picture arrived of Fertel riding around Singapore in a convertible in his gorilla costume. He was giving the thumbs-up sign. He had kept his promise.

"Anybody can buy an elephant or a tiger," he said. "Just pick up the phone and go buy them. But try to get a gorilla." In his book, Randy Fertel said his father was "odd, self-centered, and nuts." Obsessed with the animal, the Gorilla Man even named one of his racehorses Fertel's Gorilla. When the apes were at their home in the Audubon Zoo, he bought a television and put it in their domain so they could watch their favorite shows. He sat watching them for hours day after day. And when they wouldn't mate, he bought them porno tapes. Fertel passed away in 2003.

§

His answering machine says, "I eats the blues. I sleeps the blues. I is the blues." World-class harmonica player J. Monque'D once lived in a shanty in Pointe à la Hache with an outhouse and kerosene lanterns. He picked cotton and beans, cut sugar cane, pulled corn, sold produce on Louisiana 23 and Lucky Dogs in the French Quarter—where he also drove a buggy (Lindy Boggs' favorite driver)—and was a barker on Bourbon Street. Even as local musicians go, he has one of the most confusing heritages known to man: a combination of Creole-Acadian, African American, Caucasian, and Native American, which he turned into an asset as he worked different audiences.

Rodney "Get the Gorilla" Fertel ran for mayor in 1969 on the promise that he would get a gorilla for the zoo if elected. Though he lost the election, he still went to Singapore and got two gorillas for the Audubon Zoo. (Courtesy of Randy Fertel)

One of Monque'D's biggest hits, "No Doubt About It," has this refrain:

I come from the bottom land
I been rebuked, used, scorned and abused
There just ain't no doubt about it
I got a right to sing the blues

It all began at age four when his grandmother, who dipped snuff, said, "Chil', you're workin' on my last nerve." So from the top of her big brown radio, she pulled something down and handed it to him. It was a harmonica. He stuck it to his lips and blew. "I just fell in love with the sound it made, and I never did stop no more." But his grandmother, who wanted to hear pretty church songs, said disparagingly: "All he likes to play is that chitlin' eatin' music. Trash blues."

The J. Monque'D Blues Band made its debut when he was thirteen at Skateland, a skating rink in the Ninth Ward. Proud, he called his grandmother to tell her what he'd done. "Son, you'll never get anywhere playing in places like skating rinks," she said. On the fortieth anniversary of his band, playing at Rock 'n' Bowl, he told the crowd: "I wish you could see me now, Grandma. I don't play skating rinks anymore—I've graduated to bowling alleys."

His life is a travelogue—he's been to Europe thirty-eight times and to several Eastern European countries. He's played with Muddy Waters, John Lee Hooker, and Lightnin' Hopkins. He's a regular at the Blues Tent during Jazz Fest, Ruby's Roadhouse, and Rock 'n' Bowl. His trademark is his humor and his twenty-grand smile—he has a mouthful of gold that spews forth story after story, song after song. One of them, "After the Beep," is a reference to the messages he left on his ex-wife's answering machine, asking about their daughter's whereabouts. The result was him serving time for stalking—and a great song.

"He's an authentic bluesman and one of the greatest characters I've ever met," said John Blancher, owner of Rock 'n' Bowl. "Rarely do you know someone who at least once a week he pops into your head and you have a story to tell—and seldom is it the same story. The amount of material that J. Monque'D has assembled, if compiled, would rival *War and Peace*."

§

J. Monque'D is shown here performing onstage in the Blues Tent at the 2015 New Orleans Jazz & Heritage Festival. (Photo by "Da Doc dat Rocks" Mancina)

Beloved sports commentator Buddy Diliberto once said, "If the Saints ever make it to the Super Bowl, I'm going to wear a dress and dance through the streets."

The outspoken Buddy D passed away in 2005. In 2010, after the Saints had defeated Indianapolis and Peyton Manning in Super Bowl XLIV, thousands of men wore dresses and danced from the Superdome to the French Quarter with thousands watching—a fitting tribute to a master of malapropisms whose knowledge of sports was vast and who had regular characters such as Abdul D. Tentmakur, Bubba on His Magic Carpet, Sid from Jefferson, and Dr. Kevorkian calling his WWL radio show *Sports Talk*.

After an 0-5 start to the Saints' 1980 season (which ended 1-15), on his TV show, Buddy D wore a bag over his head with "Aints" on it, initiating the idea of fans wearing bags over their heads to the games and giving birth to the "Bagheads." Credit for the idea goes to Bobby LeCompte, manager and bartender for Diliberto's, Buddy D's Lounge in Metairie.

In 1982, Tulane was a heavy underdog to Orange Bowl-bound LSU. Buddy D famously said, "Tulane has as much chance beating LSU straight up as the Russians have of showing up in Kenner on Sunday." Tulane won 31-28, and on his Sunday post-game TV show with Tulane head coach Vince Gibson, Diliberto wore a Russian fur hat.

In 2003 he was roasted, and some of his best slipups were recalled: "We're going to pause ten seconds for station idefecation."

He called Snake Stabler "Stake Snabler" and Donte Stallworth "Donte Stallpepper." He talked about "torn lee knigaments," a "torn rotary cup," and boxing matches in "Levada, Nas Vegas." He turned Old Dominion into "Old Dominican." He introduced Joe Yenni the mayor of Kenner, as "Joe Yenner, mayor of Kenni." In Lake Tahoe, Buddy and lifelong pal and ex-NFL player and coach and Tulane quarterback Richie Petitbon were playing the horses at Santa Anita in a racing sports book. It was nearing dinnertime, and a waiter approached and asked Buddy if he liked abalone. Buddy looked up from his racing form and said, "What race is he in?"

The Saints sometimes led in "time of obsession." He tried to say "secondaries," but it came out, "San Diego quarterback Dan Fouts retired today after seventeen years of terrorizing NFL secretaries." In several Mardi Gras parades, the unit carrying Abdul D. Tentmakur and his band has pictures of and tributes to Diliberto—a testament to the sportscaster's enormous impact on the city.

Always a gambler, Buddy D was fond of Damon Runyon's observation: "The race is not always to the swift, nor the battle to the strong, but that's the way the smart money bets."

New Orleans native and Tulane graduate Angus Lind covered the biggest stories of the 1970s, including the Downtown Howard Johnson sniper incident and the construction of the Louisiana Superdome. But he is best known for his work for the States-Item *and the* Times-Picayune *from 1977 to 2009, when he wrote a column that took an irreverent look at the city and state, its characters, idiosyncrasies, linguistic shortcomings, and the lighter side of life. He is the author of* Prime Angus, *a collection of readers' favorite columns. He received the Press Club of New Orleans' Lifetime Achievement Award in 2010.*

Bernard "Buddy D" Diliberto, the legendary sportscaster and talk-show host for WWL-AM radio, reigned as king of the satirical Krewe du Vieux parade in 1997 with the theme "Krewe du Vieux Goes Deep." The outspoken and beloved Buddy D died in 2005, five years before the New Orleans Saints won the Super Bowl. (Courtesy of Angus Lind)

A Sense of Plates

Ian McNulty

New Orleans is not a town to push away from the table before it's good and ready. In fact, it's likely to hold on until it's a tad overstuffed. We like our po' boys with a dozen or so shrimp spilling from the loaf. We like our redfish covered with enough crabmeat to constitute a side dish. The prospect of too much food is not one to excite much angst here.

And yet, there has lately been some unease around New Orleans that perhaps the balance of things was coming undone, even for a city that customarily tilts toward more. New Orleans can't pack in enough food, but the question on people's lips, between the dabs of gravy and meunière, was if it was possible for the city to pack in any more restaurants.

Year after year now, a restaurant boom has expanded both the number and type of eateries in New Orleans and even loosened the definition of what constitutes a restaurant. Any structure with enough room for a kitchen hood and a few tables is liable to get drafted into the ranks of new restaurants now, and there are roving food trucks, one-off pop-ups, and all manner of dining-themed entertainment in between.

From high-concept showplaces to bootstrap startups, they're bringing the flavors of the world. It's a kimchi-loaded, tapas-style, Mediterranean-inspired smorgasbord, all wrapped in a tortilla, tossed in the fryer, and slashed with hot sauce.

This is the pace of the foodie frenzy that has gripped twenty-first-century America, a time when chefs are rock stars and when travel is largely an excuse to eat something new somewhere cool and send photos of it back to your envious friends. New Orleans is right there in the midst of it, connected as never before to the prevailing trends with social media and food programs at every angle. For locals who once pined for something different, it's brought an increasingly variegated menu for the plucking.

But in the background there was a note of disquiet, a concern that parts of New Orleans culture that people cherish would grow unrecognizable. It was the notion that the stampede of the new would leave in the dust those bastions that look and taste and sound like New Orleans, the ones that give that authentic feel of home. And when New Orleans no longer tastes like New Orleans, the result is cultural indigestion.

Just like everywhere else, the restaurant scene in New Orleans represents both culture and business. But it's also more than that. It is a calling and a lifestyle, a hobby, an individual compulsion, and the collective expression of a city's spirit. New Orleans doesn't just take its food and its restaurants seriously; it takes them personally. No wonder we are a tad defensive about the whole thing.

Authentic, Odd, Ours

New Orleans has long been America's gastronomic playground, a city where people draw up eating itineraries like tour schedules, maybe with some downtime thrown in for shopping or sleeping. The millions of annual tourists are not, after all, coming here to lounge on the beach or ski a great mountain. They are coming for a little something they can't get at home, something in the promise of the city's exotic otherness, its architecture and history, its tropical languor, its rumor of looser mores, and, of course, its food.

Restaurants are the great access point to the local culture, a way for people to feel intimately and intuitively what it means to be New Orleanian, at least from the vantage of our daily meals. It is an emblem of the city that is easy to share. But understanding the food and the restaurant community here takes more than a dinner reservation and a fine-tuned palate. It's a journey. That is the reason for the city's obsession, and that's the root of the reflex to buck against the idea that it's missing something that can be remedied by the next trend.

New Orleans food is delicious, it is original, it is authentic, it is odd, and it is ours.

We are protective of it because we know it could not have come about anywhere else, and we've seen how it fails to thrive when transplanted. Attempts to serve New Orleans cuisine very far from its homeland tend to be farcical or simply unsatisfying. If you have a taste for New Orleans food, then you know that when you leave New Orleans, the only part of it you can take with you are the cravings.

That is because ingredients and know-how do not constitute the whole recipe that make New Orleans cuisine feel complete.

A Fruitful Fusion

New Orleans cooking is Old World cooking carried very far from the Old World, and as it traveled the bumpy road of history, things fell in and things fell out. The result is a fruitful fusion, the unmeasured blend of tradition and compromise, thrift and plenty, time-tested ideas and the influence of a new climate with a new larder and new neighbors.

Every recounting of its history includes a few obligatory credits, mirroring the region's colonial timeline, the legacy of slavery, and the American immigrant story. It starts with the French and is joined by the Spanish. Then come the Germans and the Italians, specifically the Sicilians. Native Americans will get a nod. The more enlightened telling of our culinary heritage may laud the central but long-relegated role played by generations of African Americans running the kitchens of Louisiana, domestic and commercial. When there's time to take any of these facets beyond the basics, scholars and chefs can make their case in detail, present evidence contradicting conventional wisdom, and show more complex interconnections.

Many other regions can tell their own version of diverse peoples cooking together in the New World. It's that old handy "melting pot" metaphor. But what excites the passions of New Orleanians is not a melting pot tale.

What New Orleanians are looking for at the bottoms of their spoons and the tips of their forks is not a sum of many parts but a unique whole, not a comingling of different stories but a rendering of their own stories. They taste New Orleans food and recognize a line in the sand—this is ours, and it is different from anywhere else. There is pride in tradition and also pride that these traditions stand out starkly from others, even those of our close neighbors.

Learned and Earned

The city's cuisine is famous for its heartiness, but it comes with no guarantees. There are classic dishes and traditional ways of preparing them, but there are no codified rules or governing body, none of the controls that protect French wine or the promise of litigation that guards corporate brands. Instead, it relies on tacit relationships between the people who show up for a meal and the people who make it happen, one that goes beyond the purely commercial. It pulls on something that is part of the New Orleans identity.

It's not that every day must begin with beignets and end with a big boozy tureen of café brûlot, with a praline break in between. But the things that look like clichés on the outside still have a strong resonance for those who connect with New Orleans through its food. Restaurants themselves become part of this connection.

Business names such as Antoine's and Tujague's, Galatoire's and Arnaud's and Brennan's have become part of the city's cultural landscape, and they are meaningful to people who may not often, or even ever, dine under their roofs. Patronizing certain restaurants is a matter of personal taste, priority, and

Antoine's Restaurant is considered one of America's oldest restaurants. It was founded in 1840 and is located in the French Quarter. (Photo by Peggy Scott Laborde)

During his 1937 trip to New Orleans, Pres. Franklin Delano Roosevelt dined at Antoine's. Then mayor Robert Maestri, shown to the right of the president, asked Roosevelt, "How do you like 'dem oysters, Mr. President?" Proprietor Roy Alciatore is standing directly behind the president. (Photo courtesy of Antoine's)

The famed dish Oysters Rockefeller was created at Antoine's. (Photo courtesy of Antoine's)

Tujague's is the city's third-oldest restaurant. Located on Decatur Street, it's known for such traditional dishes as Boiled Beef and Chicken Bonne Femme as well as a contemporary Creole menu. (Photo by Sam Hanna, courtesy of Tujague's)

Galatoire's, which opened in 1905, is located on Bourbon Street, an elegant oasis amid a world-famous entertainment strip. Shown is David Gooch, who is a member of the Galatoire family. (Photo by Peggy Scott Laborde)

Ruth Ann Udstad Fertel (1927–2002) was a Louisiana businesswoman, best known as the founder of Ruth's Chris Steak Houses. Founded in New Orleans, the business developed into a worldwide franchise. (Courtesy of Randy Fertel)

budget. But they are understood as part of the city's fabric in the same way that people who don't spin jazz records at home recognize New Orleans jazz greats as part of their inherited culture as New Orleanians.

On the casual end, the city's restaurants are an extension of home cooking, preserving the stuff that New Orleans loves. When New Orleans people eat at neighborhood joints like Mandina's or Joey K's, Li'l Dizzy's or Liuzza's or the Creole destination Dooky Chase's, they are not just looking for an approximation of down-home food; they are very often actually comparing the meal to home cooking.

When New Orleans looks down at the plate, it doesn't just see trout amandine or shrimp remoulade or stewed chicken. When New Orleans looks at the plate, it sees itself. Some of this feels hereditary, as the family table is the most conducive environment to instill a food culture, and that food culture also carries through to restaurants. But New Orleans culinary citizenship isn't just handed out with your birth certificate. It must be learned, though it's not something you pick up in culinary school between knife skills and soufflé workshops.

It has to be learned by eating and cooking, by serving and dining, by working the markets and fishing the waters and talking with diners and chefs and

Mandina's, located on Canal Street in Mid-City, is known for its Creole-Italian cuisine. (Photo by Peggy Scott Laborde)

Li'l Dizzy's is one of the city's most popular Creole soul food restaurants. It's run by Wayne Baquet, whose father ran Eddie's Restaurant for many years. (Photo by Peggy Scott Laborde)

Liuzza's in Mid-City is typical of the New Orleans Italian-style neighborhood restaurant. (Photo by Peggy Scott Laborde)

Fruit and vegetable vendors were once a common sight around New Orleans neighborhoods. Arthur Robinson, known as Mr. Okra, and his family continued the tradition. (Photo by Peggy Scott Laborde)

Emeril Lagasse, shown here with Commander's Palace matriarch Ella Brennan, was the executive chef at Commander's Place from 1985 until 1990. (Courtesy of Commander's Palace)

participating in the food culture. It comes from producing and partaking, from being there for the food spreads that adjoin the holidays and for the everyday red-bean-Monday/fried-fish-Friday rhythms of this city. It's part of the celebrations that gild our joy and the succor at tragedy and loss.

Plenty of those who most prominently carry the mantle of New Orleans cuisine are adopted New Orleanians, as are many of those working the levers in the engine rooms of the dining scene. They have learned it, and they have earned it. And like generations before them, they help shape the cuisine and our dining scene and expand the framework of what it means to be a New Orleanian.

A Progression on the Plate

New Orleans cuisine has a flavor profile: rich, layered, more cooked-in soul than pristine raw beauty. But also, crucially, it has an attitude, an appreciation. It has generations behind it, memories and gratitude and context. When we talk about the texture of New Orleans food, we don't just mean how it feels in the mouth. In this case, the texture of food is a feeling that reaches back to the cortex.

The tale of New Orleans cuisine isn't a progression or a history so much as it is a condition, as ongoing and omnipresent as the belly rumbling for our next meal. There are turning points and trends, but there is no destination because it is so thoroughly subjective.

That makes it hard to pin down, but that's also what gives New Orleanians such a sense of ownership over it. That's what inspires pride and protectiveness for something that even the starkest proponents cannot claim as strictly their own. It becomes personal through our own interpretation and tastes, yet it remains genuine because it is tied to a place and a people.

There have been influential individuals, including some who changed the course of flavors and trends that mark New Orleans cuisine and who inspired next generations. There are masters of Creole flavor and queens of Creole cuisine. But not even they are the final word. There is no final word. It has to keep evolving or it stops being what it is.

And what it is, finally, is ours. It's New Orleans food, the welcome mat we lay out, the lure for visitors, the reward and balm for the everyday aggravations and the periodic epic calamities that seem a part of the bargain of living here.

Most people don't live in New Orleans because it's sensible or profitable, no more than truehearted people would marry someone for those reasons. People live here because they're in love with it. Participating in the New Orleans food culture—pulling up to the table, stepping up for the dance of the dining scene as it bends here and holds fast there, making your mark and enjoying the ride—this is all part of that romance.

Ian McNulty covers food culture and dining as a staff writer for the New Orleans Advocate, *the city's daily newspaper, and his radio commentary "Where Y'Eat" airs weekly on local NPR affiliate WWNO. A Rhode Island native, he has been eating his way through New Orleans since relocating to the city in 1999. His books include* Louisiana Rambles: Exploring America's Cajun and Creole Heartland *and* A Season of Night: New Orleans Life After Katrina.

When Misfortune Blows in the Wind

John Magill

On August 26, 1965, Hurricane Betsy formed east of Trinidad. It made a loop north of Puerto Rico, then another loop east of Jacksonville. Changing course, Betsy struck Miami before entering the Gulf of Mexico. Predicted to hit Galveston, it instead made landfall near Grand Isle at 9 p.m. on September 9. Grand Isle had wind gusts over 160 miles per hour. The eye covered Houma and New Orleans.

More than five inches of rain fell on the Crescent City, causing little problem. Storm surge lifted the Mississippi River from just over three feet to sixteen feet. While tossing ships into wharves and levees, the river did not flood the city—floods came from elsewhere.

An eerie vestige of the effect of 1965's Hurricane Betsy on the lower Ninth Ward. (Courtesy of The Historic New Orleans Collection)

Lower Plaquemines Parish went under water, something that happens in all major hurricanes in southeast Louisiana. Nearly two-thirds of St. Bernard Parish's population was left homeless. Floodwater came from the newly opened Mississippi River-Gulf Outlet (MRGO) and the Gulf Intracoastal Waterway in eastern New Orleans. From there, water funneled into the Industrial Canal. The Lower Ninth Ward flooded badly, with some people contending that the east side levee was dynamited to save the west side. This has been strongly denied, especially since the west side also flooded with up to eight feet of water.

New Orleans east of Paris Road—then called Orlandia, a proposed "city within a city" that never materialized—was inundated. West of Paris Road, subdivisions along Chef Menteur Highway stayed dry, but low land between there and the lake flooded. In a few years, this was developed as Lake Forest, the modern core of eastern New Orleans.

The storm caused seventy-two deaths here and was the nation's first billion-dollar disaster. Pres. Lyndon B. Johnson flew over the city, and soon Congress authorized a hurricane protection plan overseen by the US Army Corps of Engineers to protect New Orleans from future "Betsys."

Low-lying New Orleans is flood prone from the river, Gulf, and rain, and protecting it is a costly, challenging ordeal. The early city clung to high land along the Mississippi, with river floods the greatest fear. In 1723, the first levees were raised, and they continued to be raised higher with each successive flood into the twentieth century. Between 1735 and 1927, thirty-eight major floods occurred in the lower Mississippi valley; nine flooded the city. In 1816, water came from a crevasse in today's Carrollton while in 1849, another occurred in what is now Harahan. The latter was the last time New Orleans flooded from the river. In both cases, water reached modern St. Charles Avenue and the French Quarter. Subsequent floods such as the Bell Crevasse of 1858 and the Ames Crevasse of 1893 happened on the Westbank. During the Great Mississippi River Flood of 1927, a levee was dynamited in St. Bernard to relieve the city. Afterward, spillways at Bonnet Carré—something John McDonogh proposed in 1816—and Morganza were built to divert floods from urban areas.

The 1770s and '80s were bad times for the Crescent City. In 1778, a hurricane passed south of the city; in 1779, the eye of another passed right over town, and a third hit in 1780. Even worse came in 1788 when a fire consumed most of the city. Another fire leveled over 200 buildings in 1794. Later fires have been contained, except in 1895 when ten square blocks of Algiers burned.

The "Great Louisiana Hurricane" of 1812 blew down buildings. This storm did not flood New Orleans, but as the city grew back from the river, hurricane flooding became an issue. In 1831, the "Great Barbados Hurricane" not only sent water to Rampart Street but also broke the river levee at St. Louis Street. Three hurricanes came in 1860, the third flooding Rampart Street again. Shipping canals like the Carondelet and New Basin helped drain the city but also channeled water in. In 1871, a breach at Bonnet Carré raised water levels in Lake Pontchartrain, and strong north winds filled canals. When a drainage canal levee broke, one-third of the city flooded, reaching the business district and French Quarter. The levees were not topped, but shoddy maintenance was blamed for the breach.

After 1900, a massive new drainage system of canals and pumps drained once-uninhabitable swampland. This not only allowed the city to expand outward but also, coupled with knowledge that mosquitoes carried yellow fever, ended deadly yellow fever disasters such as the ones in 1853 and 1878; the last such epidemic was in 1905.

The Crescent City Submerged.

By the unusual overflow of the Mississippi, the river side of the city of New Orleans, Louisiana, has been submerged; in many places the water reaching as high as the second stories of dwelling-houses. The damage caused by the inundation is almost incalculable at present, but it is estimated at many millions of dollars. We have seized the occasion to give our readers life-like pictures of aquatic street scenes and incidents, such as will give them a clear idea of the general effects of the inundation, and will, we are sure both touch and amuse them.

The scene in Claiborne Street was very picturesque. A preponderance of square barges indicated timely precaution on the part of a majority, but dozens more, with their trousers rolled up to their thighs, floated about on planks and the most unseaworthy rafts. Placidly *cruising* over the troubled waters were men, boys and girls, and even women, whose air of *abandon* and generous display of personal charms was more suggestive of quiet desperation than any less worldly feeling. Many appeared undecided whether to laugh or cry, and compromised the matter by snickering at the mishaps of others, and remaining very silent in contemplation of their own adversity.

A corpulent gentleman, whose forlorn attempt to propel himself to a neighboring house on a great unwieldy log, culminated in an artistic dive, created great merriment, and it was not until he had swallowed several mouthfuls of brackish water that the hilarity ceased, and he was fished out.

Skiffs were going down Claiborne Street, and every thoroughfare above it, in numbers, and the moving of furniture quite as lively as it was in '60, while the usual sights—such as the colored man with the solitary "dorg" on a raft; the little boys in their mother's washtube

A GENERAL VIEW OF THE INUNDATION IN CLAIBORNE STREET.

having a Harvest race of their own; the auld woman with the sow and the litter of young pigs in a skiff—were visible. A cab, driven by a negro, had capsized, and Sambo, who was thereby drenched, had a good but damp time of it to right his cab again, and avoid the freely volunteered jokes of the idlers on the neutral ground, who inquired how much he would charge to go to the lake, and other similar sympathizing questions.

Then comes the dark side of the picture in the distress occasioned to the inhabitants of the quarter most affected by the overflow. Their sufferings were somewhat relieved by private charity.

Police boats, nearly all of which carried from fifty to one hundred loaves of bread, plied to and fro among the sufferers, distributing food.

Early in the morning officers were despatched to the different bakeries with directions to purchase all the bread that could be spared. The majority of the bakers had only sufficient to supply their customers, and all the workmen were absent; but by a careful selection perhaps a thousand loaves were secured, and by three o'clock they were all distributed.

Perhaps twenty boats in all were engaged in this benevolent service, and many families were not only prevented from famishing, but removed by them to places of refuge.

SCHENECTADY, N. Y., is blessed with the presence of a man "just two hours from heaven, who professes to have power to kill souls and bodies, or to breathe into dead spirits the breath of spiritual life. He says that heaven is a large city filled with beautiful mansions, and each mansion is surrounded by a large garden, in which every variety of potatoes grow with tropical luxuriance, while hell is a large lake of kerosene. Women are not immortal, and their souls can never go to heaven, as no strife can enter there. He is sane on other subjects than religion.

THIS story comes from Sharp Mountain, in Pennsylvania:

Two young girls a few days ago left a smaller one, about four years old, alone, under a tree, for a short time, and, on returning to the spot, found the little one standing still and speechless—neither replying to their questions, nor wishing to leave the spot. They finally carried her home against her will, where every question was asked, and effort made to make her speak, but in vain, until they inquired if she had seen a snake, when she immediately went into convulsions, with which she has been afflicted at intervals ever since.

BAD-IN-AGE is worse in youth.

A FATAL encounter between a sergeant of the National Guard and a Uhlan, recently occurred near Paris. The sergeant, who was drunk, approached too near the outposts of St. Denis, and met there one of the Uhlans, a bearer of dispatches, on his road to the German camp. The sight of the Uhlan excited the sergeant to such an extent, that he drew his sword, in order to bar the passage. The Uhlan drew also, spurred his horse, and killed the National Guard with a violent sword cut on the head.

ONE of the neatest toasts ever given: "Woman —the last word on our lips, because it comes from the bottom of our hearts."

PRIMITIVE NAVIGATION AND UNPLEASANT RESULTS.

POLICEMEN DISTRIBUTING BREAD TO THE WATER-BOUND INHABITANTS.

SCENES OF THE RECENT INUNDATIONS AT NEW ORLEANS.

During the summer of 1871, the Mississippi River levee broke at Bonnet Carré, causing floodwaters to rush into Lake Pontchartrain. Strong winds blew the water into existing New Orleans canals. When the canal levee broke at Hagan Avenue (now Jefferson Davis Parkway), large sections of the city flooded. "The Crescent City Submerged," The Day's Doings, *July 1, 1871.* (Courtesy of The Historic New Orleans Collection)

Negatively, drainage caused subsidence as swamps dried out, and hurricane surges became a danger to the expanding urban area. A 1909 storm flooded Lakeview and Broadmoor neighborhoods, which were still sparsely settled. Worse came in 1915 when the eye of a storm passed over Tulane University with winds gusting to 120 miles per hour. Ninety percent of buildings were damaged while Lakeview, Broadmoor, Gentilly, and Mid-City flooded.

Rain floods have historically been a problem in New Orleans. Prolonged events, such as in March 1859 and January 1881, turned bowl-like Broadmoor into a big lake. With the new drainage system, rain floods became less frequent, but prolonged rain remained problematic. The Good Friday deluge of 1927 was the benchmark event until the disastrous flood of May 3, 1978. On that day, over eight inches of rain fell in a few hours, leaving many areas underwater. Some people were stranded; others waded home. Soggy carpets and furniture were dumped along curbs in flooded areas. A resultant massive drainage project tied up South Claiborne for years. Subsequent rain events, such as in 1982 and 1995, still produced widespread flooding.

In 1947, George—an unofficial name, since official hurricane naming did not begin until 1953—struck Miami and then New Orleans with 112-mile-per-hour winds. Mostly uninhabited eastern New Orleans was inundated, as were parts of the lakefront, Gentilly, the Lower Ninth Ward, and St. Bernard Parish. The worst flooding was in Metairie, where water reached six feet. The 17th Street Canal levee was dynamited to channel it out.

New Orleans "dodged bullets" until Betsy. Afterward, there was a scary miss on August 17, 1969. Category 5 Camille devastated lower Plaquemines Parish and the Mississippi Gulf Coast. The storm surge filled New Orleans' outfall canals—17th Street, Orleans, and London Avenue—nearly to their tops. Sand boils formed at Industrial Canal levees, and three feet of water accumulated just west of the canal. Had Camille been closer—at a time when New Orleanians did not evacuate—it would have been catastrophic for the city.

There were more near misses. In 1992, Andrew flattened south Miami, aimed at New Orleans, but went to St. Mary Parish. Georges in 1998 hit Biloxi, but winds brought down countless termite-damaged trees throughout New Orleans. Isidore and Lili came a week apart in 2002. While New Orleans was spared, St. Tammany's lakefront flooded twice.

The tropical season of 2005 was terrifyingly busy. Betsy and Camille proved to be rehearsals for New Orleans' greatest disaster. Hurricane Katrina passed over Miami as a tropical storm and then swung toward Louisiana—not unlike 1947, Betsy, and Andrew. Exceptionally warm Gulf waters created a monster. At one time a category 5, Katrina's storm surge stretched from Florida to Lake Pontchartrain. As a category 3, it made landfall at Buras with 127-mile-per-hour winds at 6:10 a.m. on Monday, August 29. It then struck Mississippi.

The Mississippi River rose by sixteen feet—luckily the river was low. Along MRGO and the Gulf Intracoastal Waterway, levees collapsed, sending water into St. Bernard and eastern New Orleans. Water funneled into the Industrial Canal, overwhelming levees on both sides and flooding Gentilly, Pontchartrain Park, the Lower Ninth Ward and St. Bernard. It was 1947 and Betsy all over again.

Lake Pontchartrain rose twelve feet, filling the outfall canals, which lacked floodgates. Floodwalls failed, sending water into Lakeview, Metairie Country Club Gardens, Mid-City, Broadmoor, and Gentilly. The city's lines of defense failed miserably, as floodwalls collapsed before they were even overtopped. The defense system was poorly designed, poorly engineered, and poorly constructed—reminiscent of 1871. Over eighty percent of New Orleans flooded within hours—any part that flooded in the past flooded in Katrina.

View of a home in the Holy Cross neighborhood in the Lower Ninth Ward, 2006. Search and rescue markings have been spray-painted on the building. The failure of the city's flood protection walls in the wake of Hurricane Katrina in 2005 left more than 1,500 dead and approximately 80 percent of the city flooded. (Photograph by Stephen Wilkes, 2006. Courtesy of The Historic New Orleans Collection.)

Sunrise over an area of the Ninth Ward devastated by Hurricane Katrina in 2005. (Photograph by Donn Young, 2005. Courtesy of The Historic New Orleans Collection.)

In neighborhoods like Lakeview and the Lower Ninth Ward, near canal breaches, water came with tremendous force, ripping some houses from their foundations. Water rose rapidly, trapping people in their homes and forcing them to attics and rooftops. Water sped through subsurface drains. Geysers exploded out of manholes and flooded neighborhoods, such as around Memorial Medical Center on Napoleon Avenue, where a number of patients died. Heroic and monumental rescue efforts by first responders saved countless lives; but still, over 1,500 died in Louisiana.

Water neared St. Charles Avenue, the business district, and part of the French Quarter, recalling the floods of 1816, 1849 and 1871. In the Lower Ninth Ward and St. Bernard, water met the river levee. Except for Metairie Country Club Gardens, East Jefferson was spared this fate. But drainage pumps were ordered evacuated by Jefferson Parish President Aaron Broussard, and areas there flooded from Katrina's thirteen-inch rainfall.

Between St. Charles Avenue and the river, through Marigny and Bywater, the elevation was high enough to escape flooding. Since then, this has been dubbed the "Sliver by the River."

Approximately 35,000 people sought "shelter of last resort" in the Louisiana Superdome—which stood in floodwater. Another 20,000 fled to the Convention Center. Evacuees were stranded without food, water, electricity, or sanitation in sweltering heat. State and city government faltered badly. Shootings and uncontrolled looting occurred all over town. Numerous fires erupted. Many people who had yet to evacuate feared for their property and safety. This was being reported—sometimes incorrectly or exaggerated—by the world's media. Television viewers looked on in horror as the normally lighthearted Big Easy suffered devastating losses and municipal breakdown as it became abandoned and isolated. Although desperately needed, federal response was initially not forthcoming. It finally arrived on Friday, September 2, as military trucks filled the streets. Most residents had by then left the city. Many who remained were forcibly evacuated and scattered around the country, some never to return. Those who managed to stay lived on MREs (Meals Ready to Eat)—military food rations. Blame for the slow government response fell on Federal Emergency Management Agency (FEMA) director Michael Brown. Pres. George W. Bush memorably stated: "Brownie, you're doing a heck of a job." "Brownie" resigned under fire on September 12, and President Bush spoke to the stunned nation on September 15 from Jackson Square.

It was estimated that it would take six months to drain the city, but it took only a month. Passing south in late September, Hurricane Rita caused temporary re-flooding, but Rita tracked west, bringing havoc to southwest Louisiana and Texas.

By October, residents were slowly returning to the dry "sliver." Magazine Street thrived as the city's surviving shopping district. The fleur-de-lis became the must-have symbol of the city—and remains so. Refrigerators full of rotten food were dumped on curbsides, and some remaining at Christmas were seasonally decorated. Families retuning to damaged houses were temporarily assigned FEMA trailers while damaged roofs were covered with blue FEMA tarpaulins. Postal service was nonexistent for several months. As the city repopulated, restaurants and hotels slowly reopened, but help was in short supply since so many people had not returned. Mardi Gras went on as usual. Some were critical of this, but it was a positive step toward emotional recovery.

The Corps of Engineers came under scathing attack for the collapse of federal levees. A massive multibillion-dollar, federally financed system of levees and floodgates resulted, and the infamous MRGO was shut down. The system was tested in late August 2012 when Isaac passed south of the city. A category 1, Isaac was slow-moving and carried a big surge, but the city's defenses held. Suburbs outside the system flooded, prompting the Corps to seek protective measures for those areas.

In 2016, drainage projects continue and have made several major uptown streets impassable for years. The city's population grows as it nears its 2005 level. Some areas, like Lakeview, have experienced remarkable recovery. Elsewhere, in spite of much rebuilding, there remain crumbling houses and blocks of empty overgrown land. The Lower Ninth Ward north of St. Claude Avenue has seen new elevated houses built but remains mostly vacant—the world's enduring symbol of Katrina.

Katrina cost $108 billion and was the costliest natural disaster in US history. It is the fifth deadliest hurricane and, at its height, among the most intense. These are statistics no place wants to identify with, since they are people's lives and losses and recount the near demise of a city.

John Magill is retired as curator/historian from The Historic New Orleans Collection. His specialty is the physical development of New Orleans, a subject about which he has written and lectured extensively. A graduate of the University of New Orleans, he has contributed to such publications as Charting Louisiana, Marie Adrien Persac: Louisiana Artist, *and, with Peggy Scott Laborde,* Canal Street: New Orleans' Great Wide Way *and* Christmas in New Orleans.

Taking the Lead

Dawn Wilson

Turbulence and periods of largess mark the history of New Orleans schools. From their beginning in 1841 until now, the city's schools and the children they educate have encountered ethnic and racial conflicts, deep-pocketed benefactors, financial malfeasance, corruption, a natural disaster, and a crusading resurgence unparalleled in American history.

This traumatic journey through time arrives at marker 2018 on an upswing that no one could have imagined a dozen years ago. The days and years that followed Hurricane Katrina brought many bold actions but none as surprising as the state of Louisiana's seizure and academic turnaround of New Orleans' once-failing public schools. The state transformed those failing schools into successful charters in about ten years. Test scores have doubled, and more students are graduating than ever before.

In 2005, the state's Recovery School District (RSD) took over about 100 "failing" schools. By 2018, the RSD will have returned about fifty much-improved charter schools to school board control. Combined with the school board's portfolio of twenty-two charters and six traditional schools, the unified district will contain the most semi-autonomous charter schools in the country.

It's a model that David Osborne, coauthor of *Reinventing Government*, called a new strategy that "could well shake the foundations of American education." Osborne praised the performance of the RSD's New Orleans schools in a 2012 study titled "Born on the Bayou: A New Model for American Education." At that time, he said, Michigan, Tennessee, and Hawaii had already followed in Louisiana's footsteps.

The unification of the schools under the oversight of the Orleans Parish School Board is a once-in-a-lifetime opportunity for the city to prove that it can operate an effective urban system populated by mostly low-income students. The school system's pre-Katrina history of dysfunction, corruption, scandals, and school board bickering fueled some skepticism about the future of public education under local leadership; but as New Orleans celebrates its three hundredth birthday, school leaders are riding a wave of optimism.

In recent years, new school board members have cleaned up much of the mess left by former boards and most have supported the charter model that surveys show the majority of residents favor. Resentment still simmers among some residents, however, an attitude that still tends to seep into school board politics.

Opponents of charter schools, such as those who feel the new model favors white outsiders, often downplay their academic gains and demand a return to the neighborhood schools of the past. Parents have more choices under the charter model because of an open enrollment process, but their children may not be able to attend the closest school.

Charters are semi-autonomous, tax-supported schools supervised by individual school boards and management operators that make budgetary and hiring decisions at the school level. This new model replaces the distant, centralized one that handed down one-size-fits-all mandates to principals. Also bound by teacher union contracts, that model often prevented principals from hiring the best teachers and firing the worst. Under the new system, the school board's superintendent will provide oversight of all schools, manage the enrollment process, and recommend charter renewals or changes in operators. The superintendent will also supervise a few traditional schools.

Before Katrina, the school board supervised one of the nation's worst school districts overall, but the system also contained some stellar schools. Magnet schools such as Benjamin Franklin High School, now a charter, took students based on academic achievement, drawing them mostly from middle- and upper-income families. Many of these graduates gained entry to the nation's most prestigious colleges, but children from low-income families were trapped in schools deemed "failing" by state standards. The high-performing schools remained under school board control after the state takeover.

These kinds of divisions have marked the city's schools from the very beginning. The transfer of the region from three different nations in its first century of European settlement brought language and societal clashes that created a unique city with unusual problems. The shifts from Spanish to French to American rule in its early years challenged public schooling just as it challenged every sector of life.

Differing customs caused power struggles that led to what two scholars called a "paralyzing conflict about the goals of public education." Donald E. DeVore and Joseph Logsdon made this observation in their comprehensive history of New Orleans schools, *Crescent City Schools*, a study of public education from 1841 to 1991.

After the United States purchased Louisiana in 1803, DeVore and Logsdon say, the Americans tried to spread their brand of egalitarian public education to the city, hoping that schools would act as assimilation agents for the divergent population. Those efforts collapsed into an "ethnic quarrel" that by the mid-twentieth century had been replaced by racial conflicts.

The schools' first boom years began in 1861. John McDonogh, a rich, religious-minded bachelor, left half his fortune to educate both white and black students in New Orleans and Baltimore, his native city. After the settlement of some legal squabbles, about $1.5 million—a massive sum in those days—was divided between the two cities for educational purposes, says local historian G. Leighton Ciravolo in his 2002 book, *The Legacy of John McDonogh*.

New Orleans leaders used the money to build about thirty-five schools, most carrying McDonogh's name. Vintage photos show romantic structures of spires and gables and other ornamental devices reminiscent of medieval castles. Few of the original structures are left today, and only a handful carry his name.

McDonogh's desire for his money to be used to educate children of all races wasn't honored until the civil rights era led to the desegregation of public schools. Lawsuits finally resulted in the beginning of court-ordered desegregation of New Orleans schools in 1960. The school board resisted court orders for a few years before 1960 because an early survey of parents showed that 82 percent favored closing schools to a "small amount of integration," says *Politics and Reality in an American City*, a 1969 book written by Morton Inger.

Unlike 2005, when the state stepped in to secure the educational future of thousands of mostly black New Orleans children, Louisiana politicians in 1960 adopted a dozen laws to stop integration. When those efforts failed, vicious parent protests hit national news. Mothers threw tomatoes and shouted threats at the first black child to attend an all-white elementary school in the South.

Integration prevailed, of course, but the result was not what activists hoped to achieve. White families fled to the suburbs or private and parochial schools. This white flight left the city for decades with a crippled tax base and underfunded schools. By the dawn of the twenty-first century, ineptitude and corruption brought the system to near academic and financial collapse.

A large majority of the system's students were failing state achievement tests. Less than a third scored anywhere near grade level. Their dismal scores put them at the bottom of achievement comparisons in a state already known for having some of the lowest achievement standards in the country. School facilities were crumbling, the system was over $200 million in debt, and a stream of superintendents came and went. The final superintendent called in outside agencies to investigate payroll fraud and other corrupt practices.

Before it was over, the probe involved the FBI, the IRS, and the US Department of Education. At one point, over $70,000 in federal funds went missing.

In 2004, then-superintendent Anthony Amato told District Administration website writer Ron Schachter that as much as $100 million had been lost to fraud within the system. "There were a lot of dead people receiving checks," Amato told Schachter. "So we had employees come in personally with ID and social security numbers to get paid. When we did that, 1,500 checks were left on the table."

Dozens of school employees were indicted. Reports archived on the FBI website show that Risk Manager Carl Coleman pled guilty in February 2004 for accepting bribes of more than $150,000. He took money in exchange for awarding lucrative insurance contracts.

Corruption tainted the classroom and even the school board. In an interview with *New Orleans Magazine* a few months before he died in 2013, Amato said that when he was superintendent, a student claimed a teacher offered an A for $500. Amato's harshest critic, former school board president Ellenese Brooks-Simms, pled guilty to public bribery in 2007.

Court battles and even state legislation protected him for months, but with the system on the brink of bankruptcy, Amato eventually lost the confidence of even his strongest supporters. He resigned in April 2005.

In August, Hurricane Katrina delivered the final blow. Within days of opening for the fall semester, the storm left a tumble of mud-covered desks, chairs, and blackboards, many still containing chalked greetings of welcome for the new school year. The great majority of about 120 schools were uninhabitable. The board fired thousands of teachers and staff.

Soon after, then-governor Kathleen Blanco spearheaded the takeover. The state had threatened such action before the storm, and the devastation sealed the deal for many who had been reluctant to take drastic steps. The governor's aggressive stance angered many of her supporters in the Democratic Party. Blanco, who didn't run for reelection after the storm, told *New Orleans Magazine* in 2014: "I put a lot of political capital on the line for the children of New Orleans."

Chaos reigned for months after the takeover. RSD officials scrambled to hire teachers and locate undamaged facilities to hold classes. Students complained about inedible food and nasty bathrooms.

Schools left in the control of the school board quickly won approval to become charters because that was the fastest way they could reopen. Takeover proponent Leslie Jacobs, a former member of the Board of Elementary and Secondary Education, sought national charter operators such as the Knowledge Is Power Program (KIPP) to open RSD charter schools. With the 2007 appointment of pro-charter RSD Superintendent Paul Vallas, a turnaround specialist, more schools became charters. After his departure, Superintendent Patrick Dobard chartered the remaining district-run schools, and the RSD became the first all-charter school district in the United States.

"No city has improved this much, this quickly," says a 2015 report published by New Schools for New Orleans, a nonprofit established to aid school recovery. "Though our schools are far from excellent, this transformation has positively impacted the lives of thousands and thousands of children who would have been left behind by the old system."

The report says that in 2004 only 31 percent of New Orleans students met state grade-level standards as indicated by state achievement tests. In 2014, "that figure had doubled to sixty-two percent." Moreover, in 2000, the report says, only about half of the system's ninth graders would graduate four years later. By 2015, the rate had increased to seventy-three percent.

National measures also document the turnaround. Scores on the ACT, a college entrance exam, have improved across the board, but especially among black students in New Orleans. Educate Now!, a website that tracks educational progress, says that New Orleans black students in 2016 scored higher on the ACT than black students did statewide and nationally.

Formerly a public grammar school, Edward Hynes Charter School became a charter school in 2006 and has a working relationship with the University of New Orleans. (Photo by Peggy Scott Laborde)

The Phillis Wheatley School (formerly John Dibert Community School) is located in the Tremé neighborhood. It was named after Phillis Wheatley, a slave who became the first black female poet in the United States. It is run by the FirstLine Schools organization. (Photo by Peggy Scott Laborde)

Legislation transferring schools to the RSD required their return after recovery from academic failure. As schools have climbed from failing to a state district score of average, the 2016 legislature ordered their return as soon as a transition team determines the school board is prepared to take them.

Revitalized by $1.8 billion in FEMA construction funds, the abysmal facilities that Amato inherited in 2003 are now new or renovated structures equipped with sun-lit atriums and smart boards. Not since McDonogh's death have New Orleans students been so blessed.

Dawn Ruth Wilson, former education and government writer for the Times-Picayune, *has been writing about education for* New Orleans Magazine *since 2007. In 1986, the American Association of University Professors presented her its Higher Education Writers Award. The recipient of a Rotary Club Journalism Fellowship, she studied international politics at the School of International Studies, Bologna Center. She holds a master's degree from New York University and is currently a professor of English and government at Nunez Community College.*

The Coming of Hispanics and Vietnamese

Suzanne Pfefferle Tafur

Although New Orleans is most famous for its French flair, the city is a cultural melting pot with other well-established ethnic communities—mostly of European and African descent—that began taking shaping centuries ago. These communities have influenced our city's architecture, diversified cuisine, and calendar of celebratory events, which is packed with parades and festivals honoring various heritages.

Mama Brocato and two sons at Brocato's Ice Cream and Confectionery Parlor. The popular ice cream parlor dates back to 1905, when the young Sicilian immigrant Angelo Brocato opened his shop on Ursuline Street in the French Quarter, then a mostly Italian neighborhood. Over the years, the family moved the parlor from various Ursuline Street locations to its current place on North Carrollton Avenue in Mid-City. (Photograph by Abbye A. Gorin. Printed in 1984 from a ca. 1960 negative. Courtesy of The Historic New Orleans Collection.)

From the early part of the twentieth century to today, new cultural groups have flourished in New Orleans, including the Vietnamese and Latin Americans. They've made their presence known through lively music, philanthropic organizations, and, of course, indigenous food—all while becoming a core part of New Orleans' culture and society.

The Vietnamese began arriving in New Orleans around 1975, when Saigon fell under the control of communist forces. The late Archbishop Philip Hannan, a descendant of Irish immigrants, wanted the Vietnamese to stay together for support rather than have them separated and dispersed throughout the region. So he visited refugee camps and invited the Vietnamese to live in eastern New Orleans, where he was able to acquire subsidized apartments on a large swath of land.

Slowly, Vietnamese began moving into what is now Village de l'Est and started rebuilding their lives. Refugees also moved into communities on the West Bank. But in Village de l'Est, in particular, they were able to maintain many of the agricultural and fishing traditions that they practiced in Vietnam while also preserving other aspects of their culture—like religious and culinary practices and their language—because the area was somewhat isolated from the core of New Orleans.

They established small grocery and convenience stores, bearing signs in the Vietnamese language, along with restaurants, community development and health centers, a Buddhist temple, and a church—Mary Queen of Vietnam, where they celebrate a portion of Tet, the Vietnamese lunar New Year.

The church-based celebration includes fireworks, games for children, musical performances, and all sorts of Vietnamese food options, including *pho* and spring rolls as well as duck eggs and curried goat.

The New Orleans East Vietnamese community's weekly outdoor market, which is held in an empty parking lot on Alcee Fortier Boulevard, has also attracted folks, especially foodies, from around the city. The market takes place on Saturday mornings, before the sun has even risen, and resembles the bustling outdoor markets in Vietnam. Women wearing conical hats crouch on the ground selling various forms of produce, like bright-pink dragon fruit, and bargain with customers in what sounds like rapid-fire Vietnamese. Some vendors offer fresh seafood and livestock. Customers from within the community chat with one another, suggesting that this Saturday morning event is more than a market; it's a place where people can socialize.

The produce that is sold at the weekly market is grown in the backyards of the sellers' homes. These small urban farms expanded after Hurricane Katrina struck in 2005, when the Vietnamese community lacked access to traditional food markets and disaster relief programs. With the urban farms, they were—and still are—able to create their own food supply and practice sustainability.

Some households have even set up aquaponics systems in their backyard. This food production system combines traditional aquaculture—raising aquatic animals like koi fish—with hydroponics, which promotes the cultivation of plants in water.

Many of the refugees who moved to New Orleans during the fall of Saigon were from fishing families. They settled along the Gulf Coast, particularly in Plaquemines Parish; purchased boats; searched for business opportunities; and found success. Shrimp boats are often shared by family members and are passed down from one generation to the next.

Vietnamese restaurants throughout the city use the homegrown produce, livestock, and seafood in their cuisine. And although dining at these restaurants once required a trip to the West Bank or New Orleans East, these eateries are now seemingly everywhere. Foodies with an affinity for Vietnamese cuisine can now find *bánh mì,* a bowl of *pho,* or something more exotic, like caramelized catfish in a clay pot, in both far-flung corners of the city and in the more populated and trendy areas.

Dong Phuong Restaurant and Bakery, known for its crispy yet soft baguette bread, Tan Dinh, and 9 Roses are a few of the most popular—not to mention well-established—Vietnamese restaurants. Pho Tau Bay, which used to be located along the West Bank Expressway, closed and reopened on Tulane Avenue in the medical district in May of 2016, much to the delight of Vietnamese food fans.

This revered locale joins a host of other new East Bank Vietnamese restaurants, like Namese in Mid-City, Magasin uptown and in the CBD, and Ba Chi Canteen in the Riverbend area. Each place offers traditional menu items and dishes with a contemporary flair, along with culinary creations that showcase a fusion between New Orleans and Vietnamese cuisine.

Vietnamese-inspired items are sold at festivals, by food trucks, and in upscale restaurants. The food continues to evolve, attracting fans and a curiosity in the culture behind it along the way.

Like Vietnamese fare, various types of Latin American cuisine can be found throughout the Greater New Orleans area. Las Carnitas, a Peruvian diner in

Namese is just one example of the growing number of Vietnamese restaurants in the city. (Photo by Peggy Scott Laborde)

Kenner; Maïs Arepas, a Colombian restaurant on Carondelet; and Casa Borrega, a Mexican restaurant on Oretha Castle Haley Boulevard, are just a few examples of places serving authentic Latin American cuisine. They hint at the growing Latino population in New Orleans, which has become especially obvious in the years since Hurricane Katrina.

However, there has been a Spanish influence in New Orleans since the mid-eighteenth century, when Spain took control of New Orleans. Their presence is still palpable in the city's architecture and sometimes-spicy cuisine.

Since the Spanish occupation, there have been periods of time where waves of Latin Americans moved into the city—perhaps most notably the Hondurans, which make up the largest Latino population in the city. During the early twentieth century, major fruit companies, like Standard Fruit Company and United Fruit Company, began importing bananas into New Orleans and also brought in Honduran workers. Over time, wealthy Hondurans and students began moving into the city while others came in an effort to escape violence, political upheaval, and devastation caused by natural disasters.

After Fidel Castro gained control of Cuba in 1959, more than one million Cubans fled their country for the United States. Many of them made their way to New Orleans. Organizations like Cuba NOLA and a couple of Cuban restaurants continue to promote the traditions and cuisine of their homeland.

In the fall of 2005, following a devastating blow by Hurricane Katrina, the city experienced an influx of Latin Americans—mainly Central American, Mexican, and Brazilian construction workers, along with immigrants who took jobs in the hotel and restaurant businesses. Some established food trucks and set up shop near construction sites and hardware stores, selling tacos and Honduran *baleadas*, among other dishes. Food trucks, like Taqueria Las Delicias, are still seen rolling in and around New Orleans.

New, more mainstream food trucks, like La Cocinita, which sells Venezuelan *arepa* sandwiches, and Taceaux Loceaux, remain popular on the local street food scene.

In her book *Post Katrina Brazucas: Brazilian Immigrants in New Orleans*, Annie Gibson estimated that at one point up to 9,000 Portuguese-speaking Brazilians were living in the Greater New Orleans area. They helped with the rebuilding efforts while celebrating their Brazilian culture and developing enclaves within the city. Today, the popular Casa Samba group represents certain music and dance styles of Brazil. NOLA Capoeira teaches an Afro-Brazilian martial art that combines martial arts, dance, and music. Churra's Brazilian Grill, Brazilian Market & Café, and even Café Carmo serve dishes inspired by this vast South American country.

Other Latin American cultures have formed communities and celebrate their heritage through an assortment of festivals and events. The Nicaraguan community hosts an annual El Tope de Santo Domingo Festival, while the Colombian Volunteers of New Orleans stage holiday events and a party in July to celebrate Colombia's independence day. Members of the social organization Casa Argentina frequently gather for wine tastings and *asados*—Argentine-style barbecue dinners complete with sangria, dessert, and, of course, music and dancing.

The cultural and country borders are blurred during large events like the Hispanic Summer Fest in Laketown and Celebración Latina at the Audubon Zoo.

The New Orleans Hispanic Heritage Foundation brings together generations of Latinos, many of them successful professionals, and even Caucasians who married local Latinos. Each year, the organization hosts the Azúcar Ball, an elegant yet lively black-tie fete that offers bites from the best restaurants in

Norma's Sweets Bakery specializes in Latin American baked goods and also includes a deli. (Photo by Peggy Scott Laborde)

Dong Phuong Bakery in eastern New Orleans creates its own take on that New Orleans Mardi Gras confection, the king cake. (Photo by Peggy Scott Laborde)

Ideal Market sells many items that are popular with the local Hispanic community. (Photo by Peggy Scott Laborde)

New Orleans, live entertainment from local Latin bands like AsheSon and Julio y Cesar, and a silent auction. The proceeds benefit the foundation's scholarship program. Each year, college scholarships are awarded to young Latinos throughout the Greater New Orleans area.

Also, Puentes New Orleans and LatiNOLA aim to engage local Latinos in socio-economic and political issues while working to provide opportunities and resources for them. Spanish-speaking soccer leagues compete at Pan American and Tad Gormley Stadiums in City Park throughout the year.

Grocery stores like Norma's Sweets Bakery in Mid-City cater to the entire Latino community, although it's run by a Honduran family. They sell prepared foods, including Nicaraguan tamales, Cuban pastries and sandwiches, Honduran soups such as *sopa de marisco,* and traditional plates consisting of beans, rice, and meat or poultry. They even sell their own version of king cake, which is filled with a sweet guava paste. The grocery also acts as a gathering point for Latinos and a place where Latinos can find out about work opportunities and recreational events.

Although there are several Latino groceries spread throughout the Greater New Orleans area, Ideal Market is the most prominent, with a handful of locations. They also offer a prepared food section and a bakery full of Latin American delights, aisles stocked with imported ingredients, a butcher section, piñatas, and other party supplies. Fast-paced merengue music often plays in the background. Shopping at Ideal gives new meaning to the local term "makin' groceries," but it's an experience that's becoming more common among New Orleanians eager to learn about Latin American culture and cuisine.

A drive down a busy New Orleans street, like Carrollton Avenue, for instance, which is lined with several Vietnamese and Latin American restaurants, proves that these communities continue to thrive. And although they have preserved certain traditions and cultural identities, the distinction between their individual cultures and New Orleans culture is less obvious than it once was. One borrows traits from the other, whether it is in food or music, and ultimately makes this city more vibrant and eclectic than ever.

Suzanne Pfefferle Tafur is a New Orleans-based freelance writer and a frequent contributor to the New Orleans Advocate. *She is also the producer of two documentaries,* Latin American Cuisine in New Orleans *and* Vietnamese Cuisine in New Orleans, *which aired on WYES-TV, the New Orleans PBS affiliate. Tafur enjoys traveling, cooking, running, and exploring the rich culture of New Orleans with her growing family.*

The Sydney and Walda Besthoff Sculpture Garden at City Park. The park has made a remarkable recovery following Hurricane Katrina. (Photo by Peggy Scott Laborde)

Resetting the Clock

R. Stephanie Bruno

Gardens are the most ephemeral of human creations. Ever-changing, ever-adapting, they are subject to the mercurial whims of their keepers. But once the maker moves on—the house is sold, the keeper dies—the garden rarely survives.

I sat with Jeannette Hardy recently in a parlor of her shotgun home near the Fair Grounds and contemplated New Orleans' gardens and their evolution. Ginny, as she is known, is a longtime journalist who was the publisher of the *Vieux Carré Courier* in the 1970s and wrote news stories for the *Times-Picayune* before asking to switch to the garden beat. In 2001, she coauthored *Gardens of New Orleans: Exquisite Excess* with Lake Douglas and can be heard occasionally on National Public Radio as a commentator.

More important to me than all of Ginny's professional accomplishments are her wit, kindness, and her ardor for gardening. No matter how much I might know about gardens and plants, Ginny always knows more. As we puzzled through the approach to an essay on the flora and gardens of News Orleans at 300 years old, I posed many questions.

"Do I start 300 years ago?" I wondered aloud. "Do I explain that colonial gardens were functional rather than ornamental? And do I list the crops grown by early colonists, outline the challenges they faced? Talk about how French Quarter courtyards were places to hang laundry instead of baskets of flowers less than a hundred years ago?"

"Start with Hurricane Katrina," she answered. "It resets the clock."

Indeed it did, in so many ways beyond gardens and plantings. But the murky brown water that filled houses and swept them off their foundations also obliterated lawns, foundation beds, parterres, rose beds, vegetable patches, and even trees that couldn't manage its brackish nature. Gentilly, Lakeview, the Lower Ninth Ward, Broadmoor, parts of Old Metairie, and other neighborhoods were left more or less barren after the water receded.

In Ginny's Faubourg St. John neighborhood, the water didn't rise high enough to wash into her home, but her garden was destroyed all the same.

"All the camellias along the driveway died from drowning and the subsequent drought that killed off most plants that were not natives," she said. "What lived after Katrina were five bald cypress trees interspersed with dwarf palmettos. My old-garden roses made it, too, as did a hedge of sweet olive trees and a very old *Magnolia grandiflora*. But in between this was nothing but rubble, weeds, and the dank residue of flood waters that had risen to a foot all around my property."

The New Orleans Botanical Garden in City Park was devastated. Because of a gap in the floodwall atop the levee along the Orleans Avenue drainage canal, salty lake water poured into the 1,300-acre park and sat for weeks. When it drained away, the garden was bereft of the mature sasanqua hedges that once bordered outdoor rooms, as well as of the sweet olive allée outside of the Garden Study Center. But the resetting of the clock also brought some surprises.

"When I came back to my house, there were spindly sunflowers blooming everywhere," Ginny said. "They were the reputed progeny of birdseed scattered by the wind across the neighborhood."

Ah, yes . . . now I remember. I would find tomato plants springing up in the most unlikely places when I toured the city with out-of-town friends who wanted to understand what had happened here. (Of course, that was also when the city developed colonies of free-range chickens, some of which still inhabit areas of the Seventh Ward and Bayou Road.)

The Peggy Martin rose is an astonishing survivor of the storm, named for the woman who discovered that it had survived when she went to check on her parents in Plaquemines Parish downriver of New Orleans. The climber was the only sign of life where the home had stood. No birds and, worst of all, no people—just the rose putting out leaves and getting ready to bloom its head off.

Whether because of the national obsession with gardening or the need to strike out against the death-dealing nature of the hurricane and what we call "the federal flood," gardens began to proliferate all over town after the 2005 storm. New sod (usually St. Augustine grass) was laid, new beds installed, new soil added, and new plants took up residence.

For many gardeners, the "new" plants were the same as the plants they had lost—classics including Pink Perfection or Purple Dawn camellias, as well as Formosa or George Tabor azaleas, Savannah hollies, nandina, sasanquas, gardenias, boxwoods, and vines of Confederate jasmine. Ground covers including liriope, mondo grass, ardesia, pachysandra, and Asian jasmine re-assumed their roles in tidying up garden beds. The urge to "put things back the way they were" was irresistible after such a sudden and profound loss.

For other gardeners, the slate had been wiped clean and they were eager to try out a new look based on whatever appeared on the shelves at the big-box stores. Chief among them were Knock Out roses, developed by William Radler. Ever-blooming and disease- and drought-resistant, they were instant hits with gardeners ready for color in their chromatically depleted home environments. Since 2000, many new colors have joined the original red to enliven thousands of local garden beds.

Topiary rules the day—again (plus ça change). Never mind lines of boxwood or dwarf yaupon trimmed into neat, low hedges lining paths. Today, cones, balls, spirals, and pompoms can be found anywhere, even in modest gardens.

As patented hybrids flooded the commercial market and local gardens, the New Orleans Old Garden Rose Society mounted a campaign to convince gardeners that vintage roses were a perfect solution to post-Katrina gardens needing a rose. After all, they grow large, bloom year-round, need almost nothing in the way of care, and take on hundreds of forms. Leo Watermeier tends more than 170 of them at Armstrong Park across North Rampart Street from the French Quarter. His disciples, Jon Kemp and John Reed, have installed old roses all along the side of their Burgundy Street home, buffering their early-Creole cottage from the goings-on at Cabrini Park next door. Propagators like Don Hanson ensure that there are plenty of old roses to go around.

Orchids, day lilies, Louisiana irises, hibiscus, and bromeliads—all have champions who have promoted their propagation, hybridizing, and proliferation

A Japanese magnolia (Magnolia liliiflora) in front of this Eastlake-style cottage. (Photo by Peggy Scott Laborde)

Azaleas are among the most popular flowers grown in New Orleans. (Photo by Peggy Scott Laborde)

Civic activist Leo Watermeier has maintained an antique rose garden in Armstrong Park since 1992. The garden contains almost 175 different varieties. This is a Papa Gontier tea rose from 1883. (Photo courtesy of Leo Watermeier)

in the past decade. Carol Stauder and her cohorts in the New Orleans Orchid Society meet monthly to encourage the uninitiated to take a chance on the exotic beauties. Robert Gerlich, S. J., president of the New Orleans Chapter of the American Hibiscus Society, has collaborated with Bobby Dupont of Dupont Nursery in Plaquemine, Louisiana, to create the "Cajun" hibiscus—enormous blooms in staggering color combinations. Bryan Windham of the River Ridge Bromeliad Society manages to keep 5,000 bromeliads, adeniums (Madagascar palms), pachypodiums (desert roses), and plumerias watered, no matter how hot the summer.

Native plants have gained in popularity as gardeners were faced with repopulating their beds. "Why have a lawn at all?" some asked. "Why not native grasses? And what about planting a native Chinese fringe tree (*Chionanthus*) instead of a non-native?" Instead of tropical milkweed, native milkweed seems to be a better host plant for monarch butterflies, it was discovered, so out went the tropical and in went the native. Every sale of native plants, herbs, and butterfly attractors that Anne Barnes hosts to benefit the New Orleans Chapter of the

American Herb Society sells out before early afternoon. Certain natives perform well in rain gardens and swales (one of the newest trends in New Orleans home gardens), such as those at the Joan Mitchell Center in Esplanade Ridge and at the home of Clyde and Lizzy Carlson in Broadmoor.

Meanwhile, a fierce sense of independence seems to have developed in the hearts of some gardeners. They ask, "Why rely on retail centers for food when I can grow it myself?" Hydroponics, vegetable towers, composting, and organic gardening have all found new devotees in the city.

With so many lots in the Lower Ninth Ward bereft of homes and families, vacant land has found new uses. Close to the Mississippi River in Holy Cross, Jenga Mwendo operates the Guerilla Garden, a nonprofit community garden on Charbonnet Street where neighborhood youth can intern and learn to grow vegetables and fresh food for their families. Close to Bayou Bienvenue in the Lower Ninth Ward, Common Ground Relief uses vacant land for Cabane Coypu, a nursery that grows wetlands restoration plants: native grasses and bottomland hardwoods, including bald cypress, red maple, water oak, swamp tupelo, sweet gum, sweet bay magnolia, wax myrtle, and pecan trees. Nothing on the site is for sale; all of the grasses and trees are grown to fulfill contracts with state and federal agencies involved in wetland restoration. Just a few blocks away at the Garden on Mars, on the other hand, Jeanette Bell and Erin Zimmer grow cut flowers to sell by subscription and herbs to sell to restaurants. Their free gardening workshops teach beginners how to build, plant, maintain, and harvest a "kitchen box," the products of which can supplement purchased groceries and save on monthly expenses.

The Lower Ninth Ward isn't the only neighborhood where vacant land has been converted into gardens. In Central City, Joel Hitchcock-Tilton and Jimmy Seely started Paradigm Gardens on a vacant expanse on South Rampart Street behind St. John the Baptist church, the one with the golden steeple. They have contracts with three restaurants to provide greens, vegetables, and herbs, as well as honey from their beehives and goat milk from their small herd. Nearby, Megan McHugh and Denise Richter grow beds upon beds of flowers for the exclusive purpose of cutting and making into arrangements for parties, weddings, graduations, and other celebratory events. Their business is fittingly named Pistil and Stamen.

Somehow, despite the near total devastation at the New Orleans Botanical Garden, the garden did indeed recover, with yew hedges replacing the ruined sasanquas. Twice-yearly garden shows have resumed, as have monthly Pelican Greenhouse sales of plants propagated by volunteers. To the delight of many, a wildflower meadow sprang up near Tad Gormley Stadium not long ago, enticing pollinators as well as frolicking children.

Destruction had also visited Longue Vue House and Gardens, the grand Stern family estate near the line that separates Orleans from Jefferson Parish. Sixty percent of the total plant collection, ninety percent of its perennials, and all of its annuals died from the incursion of brackish water and the drought after the storm. But with the help of the Garden Conservancy and devoted volunteers, Longue Vue reopened to the public less than a year after Hurricane Katrina, its Ellen Biddle Shipman-designed gardens on glorious display once again.

With the rethinking of New Orleans public education since 2005 has come a reconsideration of school gardens as educational tools. Many schools now have rain gardens, butterfly gardens, and demonstration gardens, but the Edible Schoolyard NOLA installations at five local campuses operated by FirstLine Schools integrate lessons from the garden into the curriculum.

Louisiana irises at Longue Vue. (Photo courtesy of Longue Vue House and Gardens)

Although both the Parkway Partners' community gardens and the LSU AgCenter's Master Gardener program both began years before the storm, the cataclysm made their work still more vital to the renewal of community and our green spaces. Master Gardeners have transformed the grounds of libraries, public schools, and other places through their volunteerism. Parkway Partners' Tree Troopers and Green Keepers classes have sparked the restoration of the tree canopy damaged by the storm as well as an appreciation for rain barrels and on-site cisterns. Neither would have gained traction before the storm led us to question our relationship with the water that surrounds and occasionally inundates us.

As Ginny Hardy and I talked through these developments, we realized that a gardening renaissance has swept over New Orleans since those dark days in 2005. Her own garden serves as testament to the rebirth.

"I will never forget how Godforsaken the place looked when I returned a week before Christmas that year," she said. "I've been restoring the garden ever since. It is more beautiful than ever."

R. Stephanie Bruno lives in uptown New Orleans in a circa 1867 centerhall house that her parents had the good sense to buy back in 1944. She writes about local architecture, neighborhoods, and gardens for the New Orleans Advocate *and authored* New Orleans Streets: A Walker's Guide to Neighborhood Architecture. *She attended Isidore Newman School and then Wellesley College, where she majored in English. Her garden—like her home—remains a work in progress.*

The famed Longue Vue House and Gardens Oak Allée shown after Hurricane Katrina. (Photo courtesy of Longue Vue House and Gardens)

Longue Vue House and Gardens' Oak Allée has bounced back from 2005's Hurricane Katrina in an impressive way. (Photo courtesy of Longue Vue House and Gardens)

The Deltaic Metropolis During New Orleans' Third Century

Richard Campanella

Imagine it's the early 1970s, and you're the proud owner of a new split-level in a trendy subdivision in Metairie, an area to which seemingly half of New Orleans had been moving recently. You pull into the driveway one evening, unlock the front door, turn on the light—and suddenly an orange flash materializes overhead, erupting into a fiery explosion. The house is destroyed, neighboring structures are damaged, and the blast breaks windows a mile away. You are lucky to be alive.

At least eight times between 1972 and 1977, well-maintained suburban homes just west of Transcontinental Drive exploded in this manner. "Scores of Metairie residents," reported the *Times-Picayune*, "wondered whether they are living in what amounts to time bombs."

The proximate cause for the terrifying incidents was broken gas lines, and they were resolved by new building codes requiring flexible gooseneck utility connections. But the ultimate cause was more challenging, more troubling, and more deeply rooted—literally. It was soil subsidence: the gradual consolidation and sinkage of the land surface, which in these cases cracked concrete slab foundations and severed the gas lines. New codes would mitigate this problem by requiring a grid of pilings driven into deeper, more consolidated soils to undergird and stabilize the foundations. But this of course did not prevent the rest of the neighborhood and metropolis from sinking vis-à-vis rising seas—an environmental problem a century in the making with the capability of un-making seven millennia of geology and threatening the very existence of New Orleans.

Southeastern Louisiana is almost entirely a product of an uncontrolled lower Mississippi River, which, once it flowed past the confines of its valley, lunged to and fro across two hundred littoral miles and deposited sediment on the Gulf of Mexico seafloor at a pace faster than currents could sweep them away. What resulted was that most dynamic of all coastal environments, a fluvial delta, whose continued existence demanded steady doses of fresh water and depositions of new sediment.

To humans, this fluid environment beckoned even as it forbade. New Orleans' geographical triumphs and troubles began in 1718, as Bienville surveyed the Bayou St. John portage between Lake Pontchartrain and the Mississippi River. Despite the precarity of this swampy and flood-prone site, its geographical situation—that is, how it connected with the rest of the world—seemed enticingly strategic. A city here, on the fertile banks near the mouth of North

114

America's greatest river, would perfectly position French colonials to defend and exploit the unknown riches of the vast Mississippi Valley. Competing sites were either more precarious or less strategic. Should New Orleans be built on the safest site, despite its inconvenience? Or should it exploit the most strategic geographical situation, despite its risk? Bienville opted for the latter, setting the stage for three centuries of environmental blessings and curses.

Freshwater represented both blessing and curse: the sheer volume of the Mississippi River provided superlative navigational access as well as productive ecological and agricultural environs, not to mention abundant water for domestic and industrial use. But when springtime river stage ran higher and stronger than rudimentary levees could restrain, it also periodically flooded the city, starting in 1719, with the worst crevasses occurring in 1816, 1849, and 1871. New Orleanians throughout the 1700s and 1800s feared not hurricanes and Gulf waters as the source of potential flooding but rather the Mississippi, and they made it a local priority to prevent crevasses. The levees they erected, as well as later floodwalls, barriers, gates, canals, and pumps, represented the imposition of rigidity upon an environment that was fundamentally fluid. These engineering devices enabled the creation of a great city. They also obstructed the deltaic processes that created its underlying geography.

New Orleanians additionally feared the backswamp, that water-logged *prairie tremblante* that restrained urban expansion and, according to the miasmatic theories of the day, caused yellow fever and other epidemics. "This boiling fountain of death," wrote one anonymous resident in 1850, "is one of the most dismal, low and horrid places on which the light of the sun ever shone. And yet there it lies under the influence of a tropical heat, belching up its poison and malaria." In fact, it was the *Aedes aegypti* mosquito that spread the yellow fever virus, and it mostly bred in cisterns. But this was not understood at the time, and blame instead went to what the above writer called "the dregs of the seven vials of wrath." If New Orleanians of the nineteenth century could have two wishes to improve their environment, most probably would have chosen sturdy levees along the river and the drainage of the backswamp.

Both wishes would come true over the turn of the twentieth century. In 1879, the task of controlling the Mississippi River transferred to the federal government, and the Army Corps of Engineers proceeded to realign and strengthen riverfront levees. The effort largely ended the era of Mississippi River crevasses flooding of the city proper. But it also precipitated new problems.

For one, a completely controlled Mississippi could no longer infuse its deltaic plain with freshwater and sediment; despite that, the sea would continue to gnaw away the coastal periphery. The land-building capacity of the river started to give way to the land-eroding capacity of Gulf waters—which were gradually rising.

For another, the Army Corps of Engineers starting in the 1880s adhered to a "levees-only" policy in controlling the Mississippi under the theory that a straightjacketed river would scour out its bottom and create channel space for excess water that otherwise would have flooded land. In fact, the river dropped a portion of its suspended sediment into the bedload and *raised* its bottom, which thus raised the top of the river, which required levees to be heightened, which iterated the cycle. Higher and stronger grew the levees, and the entire channel rose dangerously above the deltaic plain. It was just a matter of time before an epic high-water event would overwhelm the system, and that came with the Great Mississippi River Flood of 1927. New Orleans was spared, but anxious commercial interests nonetheless persuaded reluctant federal authorities to dynamite a levee below the city to relieve pressure on the city's flood defenses. The resulting manmade deluge upon the lands of rural folk in St. Bernard and Plaquemines Parishes, which in retrospect proved unnecessary, is remembered with bitterness to this day. The blast also decisively ended the levees-only policy, and subsequent congressional acts led to the creation of spillways and water storage reservoirs as safety valves for high-water events—a wise and hard-learned concession to the natural will of the river.

While federal departments brought the Mississippi under control, city officials endeavored to finally solve the "problem" of the backswamp. It was the 1890s, and the Age of Engineering joined forces with spirit of the Progressive Era to bring forth a series of massive municipal modernizations for water treatment and distribution, sewerage, transportation, urban beatification, and, most significantly, drainage. Following research and design during 1893 to 1895 and financing in 1899, the newly formed New Orleans Sewerage and Water Board installed a world-class urban drainage system. It would use natural topography to guide runoff to low spots through underground pipes and canals, at which point gigantic pumps would push the runoff out newly excavated and/or widened outfall canals and into surrounding water bodies.

It worked. Rainwater was jettisoned instead of accumulating in the lowlands,

This 1861 lithograph by John Bachman, titled Birds Eye View of Louisiana, Mississippi, Alabama and Part of Florida, *dramatizes how the prograded Mississippi River deltaic plain extends beyond the rest of the Gulf Coast, a product of the enormity of the river's water and sediment volume vis-à-vis the Gulf of Mexico's relatively weak tides and currents.* (Courtesy of the Library of Congress)

NEW ORLEANS. LA. AND ITS VICINITY.

This 1863 perspective, titled New Orleans, La. and Its Vicinity, *by J. Wells, W. Ridgway & Virtue & Co., illustrates how urbanization at that time occurred exclusively on the higher ground of the river-abutting natural levees, while low-lying backswamps remained undrained and undeveloped. This would change after the turn of the twentieth century, forever transforming New Orleans' urban geography.* (Courtesy of the Library of Congress)

groundwater dropped, and the scorned backswamp became valuable real estate. Everyone viewed it as a triumph: Developers could now build thousands of houses, banks could lend mortgages, families could finally escape the cramped old city and enjoy modern California-style subdivisions suited for the automobile, and the city would collect vastly more real estate taxes. Residents moved *en masse* into places like Lakeview and Gentilly, confident their world-class infrastructure had neutralized topographical and hydrological restraints. So secure were New Orleanians in their technological salvation that the tradition of building houses raised on piers faded in favor of cheaper concrete slabs laid at grade.

Drainage, however, also came at a cost. It removed water from the soil body, which allowed organic matter to decompose. Fine silt and clay particles settled into the air cavities, compacting the soil and lowering its elevation. Starting in the early 1900s, parts of New Orleans began to subside, for the very first time, below sea level. Pumps, originally positioned behind the populated area but now surrounded by it, expelled runoff into the lake through outfall canals, which increasingly rose above the sinking adjacent neighborhoods—whose populations grew. While the vast majority of New Orleans' 287,104 residents lived above sea level in 1900, only 48 percent remained above sea level in 1960, when the city's population peaked at 627,525. Fully 321,000 New Orleanians by this time resided in modern subdivisions built on lakeside lowlands now five to eight feet below sea level. Subsequent decades saw white flight followed by a larger middle-class exodus, and the same swamp-drainage-soil-subsidence cycle occurred in places like Metairie, New Orleans East, and the West Bank. By 2000, only 38 percent of the city's population resided above sea level and 50 percent of the entire metropolis south of Lake Pontchartrain lay below sea level.

Previously shaped like a crescent for its foundation upon the higher banks of the curvaceous Mississippi, New Orleans in the twentieth century drained its backswamp and spread laterally, no longer confined to natural high ground. But the drainage and sprawl brought forth soil subsidence and increased flood risk, with devastating consequences. This aerial photograph dates from the late 1960s, when suburban sprawl was in full swing. (Courtesy Richard Campanella, personal collection of NOPSI/Entergy photographs)

Lake Pontchartrain at sunset. (Photo by George Long)

A view from the top of the pedestrian bridge at Crescent Park, located along the Mississippi River in the Faubourg Marigny neighborhood. (Photo by George Long)

A century of coastal manipulation, meanwhile, had brought Gulf waters to the door of the sinking metropolis. Three major navigation canals—the Industrial (1918-1923), the Gulf Intracoastal Waterway (1930s-1940s), and the Mississippi River-Gulf Outlet (1958-1968)—were excavated to expand leasable wharf space or streamline port access. But the waterways also allowed saltwater to lap the rim of the bowl-shaped metropolis. The salinity killed cypress swamps such as Bayou Bienvenue and turned marsh into open water. Similarly, a network of roughly 10,000 linear miles of oil and gas extraction canals throughout coastal Louisiana increased the number of land/water interfaces and thus opportunities for erosion, saltwater intrusion, and swamp die-off. Their attendant guide levees and spoil banks channelized storm surges and impounded salt water.

As a result of these factors, as well as the leveeing of the Mississippi and other variables, coastal Louisiana has lost over 1,900 square miles of land in the past eighty years, a pace twenty times swifter than the Mississippi took to build those areas over the previous 7,200 years. Coastal wetlands protect New Orleans because they buffer hurricane-induced Gulf surges from reaching the city. That their disappearance directly threatens New Orleans was evidenced all too clearly in 2005, when Hurricane Katrina's surge penetrated five manmade navigation and drainage canals, ruptured flimsy federal floodwalls, became impounded in man-caused below-sea-level bowls, and led to the deaths of 1,500 people.

New Orleans endures many other environmental and geographical problems. Soil lead may be found in dangerously high levels in the urban core, left over from the days of leaded gasoline and lead-based paint, and may imperil the cognitive development of children raised in those neighborhoods. The century-old water treatment and distribution system is prone to weak pressure and leaks, leading to frequent water-boil advisories. River-water quality is marginal for domestic use, and its excess nutrients create algae blooms in the Gulf of Mexico, which in turn die, sink, decompose, and use up oxygen, creating a vast "dead zone" in the middle of one of the world's greatest fisheries. Within city limits, at least two major housing developments have been built on former municipal dumps, one of which, Agriculture Street, has since become an EPA Superfund site. Residents of neighboring parishes complain of potential health effects of malodorous petrochemical industries, and the entire Gulf Coast stands at risk from oil spills such as the British Petroleum Deepwater Horizon rig explosion of April 2010, which sent millions of barrels of crude into Louisiana marshes.

Serious as these problems are, they are generally comparable to those found in peer cities, and, chronic rather than acute in nature, they undermine the quality rather than the existence of local life. Not so soil subsidence, coastal erosion, and sea level rise: this troubling trifecta uniquely and existentially threatens New Orleans and the communities of southeastern Louisiana, particularly since the same warming climate that is swelling the seas may also increase the frequency and/or power of tropical storms. To be sure, other coastal cities confront some lesser combination of these challenges, namely sea level rise, but New Orleans is the only metropolis on the continent—and among the few on the planet—to suffer all three intensely and extensively. If current trends continue, the city by its 400th anniversary may well be a Venice-like island surrounded by Dutch-style super-barriers and surviving on a boutique economy selling a colorful past.

In some ways, it's already all that.

There is hope. Unlike other imperiled coastal areas, southeastern Louisiana brings to bear the world's greatest land-building machine, the Mississippi River. Diverting its water into rural marshes can restore at least one of the two inputs needed by fluvial deltas: pulsations of freshwater pushing back encroaching saltwater. As for the other input, sediment, there is unfortunately not enough alluvium in the water column for diversions to create much new land (the necessary particles get trapped behind upriver reservoirs or are otherwise dumped uselessly onto the continental shelf). Diversions also affect the fishing economies of St. Bernard and Plaquemines Parishes, as the freshwater radically alters salinity regimes, drives optimal oyster production farther out, and pollutes coastal marshes. Residents in those areas tend to be anti-diversion and advocate instead for the restoration of barrier islands. Everyone seems to agree that the dredging and siphoning of sediments from the river bottom into targeted areas is critical to coastal restoration, but such new land begins to subside as soon as the pumps and pipes are relocated. Legal complexity, financial costs, engineering challenges, conflicting scientific research, and resistance to expropriation make the challenge of coastal restoration promethean in its size and herculean in its execution.

Toward that end, the state Coastal Protection and Restoration Authority (CPRA) has developed a plan for scores of diversions, sediment siphons, shoreline stabilizations, and barrier island restorations at a price tag of somewhere between $50 and $100 billion. As of this writing, CPRA now, finally, has a few billion dollars in its budget to get to work. (The source of those moneys? British Petroleum, courtesy of federal fines and a lawsuit settlement—a case of disasters funding disaster recovery.)

As for urban subsidence, it has no true cure. It is not feasible to "reinflate" city soils while urban life continues above, although it is beneficial to restore groundwater so as to reduce or eliminate future sinkage. This may be done by slowing the movement of runoff across the cityscape through features such as bioswales, allowing rainwater to soak the ground through porous surfaces, and storing as much rainfall as possible in retention ponds rather than pumping it out. Post-Katrina building codes now require that new houses be raised by at least three feet—a policy that is as wise as it is humbling, in that this had been a standard practice locally since the early eighteenth century until it was abandoned in the mid-twentieth century. The exploding houses of Metairie in the 1970s, built on brittle, cracking concrete slabs, dramatically attest to this folly.

New Orleanians today have a split sensibility on the urgency of coastal restoration. Most now recognize that, over the long run, as goes the coast, so goes New Orleans. But because the $14.5 billion Hurricane & Storm Damage Risk Reduction System—that is, the improved levee system built in the wake of Katrina, another case of disasters funding disaster recovery—provides protection from the so-called 1-percent storm, residents living "inside the wall" have gained a new lease on life, at least for the next generation or two. Residents of the metropolis today worry less about geography and the environment than they did immediately after Katrina, and the flooding caused by Hurricane Isaac in 2012 was almost entirely "outside the wall," in neighboring Plaquemines and St. John the Baptist Parishes.

But we should be wary of false senses of security, for they have misguided us before. If New Orleanians go into their fourth century with one geography lesson from the prior three, it ought to be that a healthy deltaic plain is a fluid and dynamic environment, and too much of the rigid engineering that enabled the city to flourish in the first place can also undermine its geography in the end.

Richard Campanella, a geographer with the Tulane School of Architecture, is the author of nine books and scores of articles about New Orleans. The only two-time winner of the LEH Book of the Year Award, Campanella has also received the Louisiana Literary Award, Williams Prize, and Tulane Honors Professor of the Year. In 2016, the government of France named Campanella a Knight of the Order of the Academic Palms.

CHILDREN IN ST. VINCENT'S INFANT ASYLUM, NEW ORLEANS, ATTENDED BY SISTERS OF CHARITY.

Incidents of its Horrors in the Most Fatal Districts of the Southern States, *September 28, 1878,* Frank Leslie's Illustrated Newspaper. *Scenes of people stricken with yellow fever in New Orleans, Memphis, and Vicksburg. The almost annual visitation of yellow fever in nineteenth-century New Orleans took thousands of lives. Over 7,800 people died in New Orleans during the epidemic of 1853. Reportedly over 20,000 people in the Lower Mississippi Valley died of the fever in 1878. New Orleans suffered its last yellow fever epidemic in 1905.* (Courtesy of The Historic New Orleans Collection.)

Local Medicine's Biggest Battle

Brobson Lutz

New Orleans is a city branded by pestilence. Yellow fever, the queen of fatal infectious diseases, was a frequent summer visitor for our first 200 years. Cholera and smallpox were reoccurring unwelcome guests. Fast-forward to the past 100 years. Not to ignore cardiovascular diseases and other medical maladies such as tragic institutional changes after Hurricane Katrina, three diseases have helped define health care in New Orleans over the past century. They are cancer, asthma, and AIDS.

Cancer includes over 150 distinct diseases caused by cell division going amok. We sit in what some call "cancer alley," those parishes hugging the Mississippi River between Baton Rouge and New Orleans, studded with chemical and oil processing plants. Actually, except for cigarette-generated lung cancer, our cancer rates are not significantly higher than other areas of the country. Think "cancer" in New Orleans, and the name Dr. Alton Ochsner Sr. comes to mind. Ochsner made many contributions to medicine. One was to perfect a radical chest surgical procedure that prolonged life for some people with lung cancer. But the number-one medical myth in New Orleans is that Ochsner discovered the link between cigarette smoking and cancer. He never made that claim. His publications referenced work by others going back decades that linked tobacco smoke to lung cancer. Ochsner's early and tireless war against the evils of tobacco and the medical empire that bears his name are his most important legacies.

Before widespread Pap testing, advanced cervical cancer was common. Dr. Manuel Garcia was a pioneer radiation oncologist at Charity Hospital. He had thirty to forty beds for women undergoing radiation therapy for cervical cancer in the early 1940s. In his later years, Garcia handed off his practice to Dr. Joseph Schlosser, his student and a talented researcher and clinician. "Dad had the first cobalt unit in the South, even before MD Anderson," said Dr. Jayne Gurtler, Schlosser's daughter and a respected medical oncologist. Schlosser practiced at Charity for decades while also seeing private patients in an old house on St. Charles Avenue until 1988. Rumor was that when Schlosser turned on his equipment, the lights on that entire block of St. Charles would dim.

In the middle of the twentieth century, persons with advanced malignant melanoma flocked to New Orleans from all over the world to see Dr. Edward Krementz. He and his Tulane colleagues devised regional perfusion in the 1950s. They would surgically create a loop between the artery feeding a tumor and its venous return. Then, using a pump, a sectioned-off area of the body could be infused with high-dose chemotherapy.

The five founders of the Ochsner Foundation Hospital inspect blueprints for the new hospital in Jefferson Parish. They include Drs. Alton Ochsner, Guy Caldwell, Edgar Burns, Frances E. "Duke" LeJeune Sr., and Curtis Tyrone. (Artist unknown. Photograph by R. Fantazzi, 1953. Courtesy of The Historic New Orleans Collection.)

Surgery and radiation were the cornerstones of cancer treatment until the early 1960s. Chemotherapy, meaning "the use of chemicals to treat disease," came later. "We only had drugs for lymphomas and acute leukemias when I started practice at Southern Baptist in 1961," said Dr. Charles Brown, the late esteemed New Orleans oncologist. "Chemotherapy for the solid tumors came later."

No other hospital in the South has handled mass disasters like Charity Hospital. The New Orleans asthma epidemics are a prime example. Several times a year beginning in the 1950s, dozens of gasping and wheezing adults would flock to Charity. Chairs and gurneys lined the walls with "respiratory cripples." Staff doled out various treatment modalities based on age, medical history, and severity. Hydration was key, and the nurses passed out bottles of water like candy at Halloween. Newly minted interns and residents administered breathing treatments, medications, and intravenous infusions. Most patients improved over a few hours, shed their hospital gowns, and returned home. Others stayed overnight. A few were actually "kept," Charity lingo for a formal admission to the hospital. A few stragglers might appear a couple of days later, but these asthma epidemics usually abated after 48 hours.

Lung specialists initially blamed weather changes and swamp winds with fungal

Constructed in 1939 during the Great Depression, Charity Hospital on Tulane Avenue ranked among the largest hospitals in the nation. The Charity Hospital system, the second oldest in the United States, dates back to the 1730s. Heavily damaged, the hospital did not reopen after Hurricane Katrina in 2005. (Photograph by unknown photographer, circa 1950. Courtesy of The Historic New Orleans Collection.)

spores. Then a Tulane researcher pointed a finger at fumes from underground rubbish fires in New Orleans East. The Agriculture Street garbage dump fires were extinguished, yet the outbreaks continued. In 1968, Dr. John Salvaggio, an immunologist, focused on ragweed, calling it a "manmade pollutant" that "only flourishes where civilization has crept in. You never find it in the marshes." But ragweed pollen counts failed to correlate with the outbreaks. "We currently postulate that New Orleans epidemic asthma does not involve a point source chemical or particulate pollutant," Salvaggio wrote in 1971.

During my years of training at Charity Hospital in the mid-1970s, the asthma epidemics had dwindled. Still, once or twice a year, one would suddenly occur. Of course, people still have asthma attacks, but New Orleans asthma epidemics stopped completely in 1977. The mystery was solved almost twenty years later by way of Spain. Barcelona starting having epidemic asthma outbreaks after us, and geographic clustering pointed to their harbor. During thirteen consecutive Barcelona asthma epidemics, ships had unloaded soybeans at a silo lacking any filter to contain the dust. Immunological testing confirmed soybean allergies among the asthma sufferers.

The Barcelona reports triggered a look back at the extinct New Orleans asthma epidemics. Epidemiologists from Atlanta combed over Port of New Orleans archives for lists of grain-carrying vessels, arrival and departure dates, and cargo contents. They correlated ship-loading data with old weather service records showing wind speed and direction and published their findings in 1997. The asthma epidemics coincided with loading soybeans and specific wind conditions. There was no association with wheat and corn. This research solved the mystery of why our epidemics suddenly vanished. A spark ignited a grain-dust explosion that killed thirty-five Westwego workers and destroyed giant silos used to hold grains in December 1977. Rebuilt grain elevators incorporated features to avoid further explosions by decreasing grain-dust clouds. Nearly two decades later, the dots were connected. Dust-control measures instituted to decrease the risk of grain explosions ended the New Orleans asthma epidemics.

Unlike epidemic asthma, an infectious disease epidemic that debuted just over thirty years ago is unlikely to disappear any time soon. It emerged in the early 1980s with concern and confusion. Development of a blood test for the virus led to panic and protests. Finally, effective drugs began appearing in 1997. Like yellow fever and cholera in past centuries, AIDS debuted in port cities. New York, San Francisco, and Los Angeles were the 1981 epicenters. New Orleans only had five cases of reported AIDS by July 1983, according to state health statistics. As elsewhere, the disease here first occurred in gay white men. Even before there was a specific blood test for AIDS, groups at risk grew to include hemophiliacs, injection drug users, Haitians, and recipients of blood transfusions.

The first case I treated was at Southern Baptist Hospital in 1982. The man was in an intensive care unit. In his room was a nurse, fright in her eyes, garbed in layers of protective gowns and masks. While much was unknown about AIDS at the time, the epidemiology was clear. This was an infectious disease but not one with airborne transmission. Dr. Ewing Cook, a pulmonologist, and I arrived about the same time. We examined the man without any protective gear. Cook wrote orders to manage his respiratory distress, and I ordered antibiotics for pneumonia. By the next day, the hospital staff were treating him like any other patient with pneumonia but with needlestick precautions, a good idea for any caregiver-patient contact.

Physicians in New Orleans have care of infectious diseases embedded in their DNA from the days of smallpox, yellow fever, and cholera epidemics. Except for a few instances, the fear of treating people with AIDS never gripped the New Orleans medical community as it did in some other cities. One New Orleans dentist did refuse to clean the teeth of two HIV-positive patients in 1993, which turned into a $120,000 federally imposed fine under the Americans with Disabilities Act.

Pharmaceutical advances and governmental assistance seemed slow in the 1980s and 1990s. They *were* slow. Volunteers founded community groups such as NO/AIDS Taskforce and Buzzy's Boys to meet unfunded social needs. Arthur Jacobs, a retired policeman, donated use of a small building that served as the first NO/AIDS walk-in office on Bourbon Street next to his Clover Grill. But people kept dying. In the early days of the HIV epidemic, it was not unusual for patients from most of Louisiana and the lower half of Mississippi to come to New Orleans for treatment.

Some patients with known HIV infections unwisely delay taking effective medications to preserve their immune systems. At one time New Orleans even had a community-based and state-sanctioned "CD4 clinic." It provided free and anonymous blood testing every few months, allowing individuals with HIV to monitor the destruction of their immune systems over years in the misguided belief that treatment was best delayed until "it was really needed." People diagnosed and treated in a timely fashion do well. While there remains no cure for HIV infection, daily medications can keep the virus suppressed and the immune system functional. But the medications used to control the disease can cause cardiac, kidney, and other complications.

AIDS has killed about 6,000 New Orleanians since 1983, but the epidemic

The state of the art University Medical Center opened in 2015. (Photo by Peggy Scott Laborde)

The Southeast Louisiana Veterans Health Care System Medical Center opened in New Orleans in 2016. (Photo by Peggy Scott Laborde)

has not abated. Even more people calling the Crescent City home today are infected than have died since our city's first known death in 1982. New Orleans holds a bronze medal for the number of citizens per capita living with HIV. Our metropolitan area is number three in the United States. Our sister city Baton Rouge has the gold medal for first place in 2016. Louisiana had about 1,000 new HIV infections in 2015, and over 300 of those were from New Orleans. New infections have shifted from gay white men to urban young adults and especially youth of color. Poverty, poor education, religious oppositions to condoms, delayed access to Medicaid, scant state funding, and less-than-aggressive grant-seeking by our health departments are factors that fuel this preventable disease.

New Orleans was a powerhouse for medical care and research for our first 250 years. Our leading edge began to fade when some of our best medical minds migrated to other places, such as Dr. Michael DeBakey to Texas. Birmingham, a city without a four-year medical school until World War II, recruited innovators such as Dr. John Kirklin, along with his research and support staff from the Mayo Clinic. As we enter our fourth century as a city, New Orleans can reclaim its lost position as a leader in medical care, research, and treatment. This ascension will take more than new buildings. Bring in the medical stars with their supporting casts, and the infrastructure will follow.

Brobson Lutz moved from Alabama to New Orleans to attend medical school and never left. After internal medicine and infectious disease training at Charity Hospital, he headed the city of New Orleans' Health Department under three mayors. For two months after Hurricane Katrina, he helped staff a sidewalk medical clinic on Dumaine Street dubbed the City Health Department in Exile. He practices internal medicine in uptown New Orleans with his longtime partner, Dr. Kenneth Combs.

This Storied City

Susan Larson

New Orleans is known for many arts—literature, music, cuisine—but perhaps its greatest art form is transformation. Washday becomes "red beans and rice Monday," leftover bread becomes *pain perdu*, *papier-mache* and glitter become the fantastic spectacle of Mardi Gras, and ordinary people become extraordinary writers.

Some writers have literally changed their identities here: William Sydney Porter, on the lam from embezzling charges in Texas, became O. Henry. Samuel Clemens ventured down the river, heard a common maritime expression, and adopted Mark Twain as his pseudonym. Thomas Lanier Williams discovered a certain "flexibility in his sexual nature" during a visit and went from Tom to Tennessee. See what I mean? Transformation!

Perhaps only New Orleans could have turned a shy Catholic schoolgirl into Anne Rice, who presides over an entire fictional universe of vampires and witches. This city gave Walker Percy, an ailing MD, the inspiration for philosophical novels that raise enduring existential questions. Then there's the story of John Kennedy Toole, a talented English teacher who saw through to the comic heart of the city in *A Confederacy of Dunces* but took his own life in despair, never seeing his great work receive its rightful acclaim.

Three hundred years of literature have brought us to a moment where images of New Orleans are firmly embedded in the collective consciousness. Images of the city—beautiful buildings, great oak trees, streetcars, brass bands, colorful Mardi Gras parades, views of the mighty river—have a way of taking hold in the heart. Many visitors, arriving for the

Left: *Mark Twain (Samuel Clemens, 1833-1910) and New Orleans-born George Washington Cable (1844-1925) both drew heavily upon life on the lower Mississippi for their novels and short stories.* (Photograph, n.d. Gift of Mr. Al Rose. Courtesy of The Historic New Orleans Collection.)

Tennessee Williams (1911-1983) on a wooden bench in front of the La Branche Building at the corner of Royal and St. Peter streets in the Vieux Carré. Williams lived in New Orleans, his "spiritual home," off and on from the late 1930s until his death in 1983. (Photograph © by Christopher R. Harris, 1977. Courtesy of The Historic New Orleans Collection.)

first time, speak of a sense of *déjà vu*. Does this come from having read and loved such well-known literary works as *A Confederacy of Dunces, The Moviegoer, A Streetcar Named Desire, Interview with the Vampire,* or *The Awakening,* those classics of the canon? Or seeing the many movies filmed here? Maybe.

This familiarity could also have come from the nightly news, for few cities have faced down a disaster in the style in which New Orleans faced Katrina, an epic event not only in the personal lives of individuals or in the ongoing story of a great American city, but in the history of our country, as well. Perhaps resilience and storytelling—constructing the common narrative—are intertwined.

After all, a literary bent goes back to our shaky beginning. From the city's very founding in such an inhospitable landscape, writing came out of New Orleans. Explorers and early settlers kept journals and wrote letters, chronicling the evolution of the city that has been variously described as accidental, improvisational, and—more recently—doomed. Early writers made the most of cultural complexity and local color. One of the first publications of note to come out of New Orleans was *Les Cenelles* (*The Hawthorns*), published in 1845, the first anthology of poetry by African Americans to be published in the United States.

The mid to late nineteenth century was a busy time. Kate Chopin lived in New Orleans from 1870-79 and still captivates audiences with *The Awakening,* an early feminist classic. The World's Industrial and Cotton Centennial Exposition of 1884 inspired considerable high-profile magazine editors and journalists to visit. Readers' interest was piqued by writers such as George Washington Cable (*Old Creole Days, The Grandissimes*), who wrote about social injustice as he saw it, inspiring a feud with and the career of Creole apologist Grace King (*New Orleans: The Place and the People, Memoirs of a Southern Woman of Letters*). Meanwhile, roving journalist Lafcadio Hearn extolled the charms of his adopted hometown in works such as *Chita, Gombo Zhebes,* and *La Cuisine Creole.*

New Orleans has had many so-called golden ages in its literary history, but the 1920s were especially lively. Sherwood Anderson was in residence in the Pontalba Buildings, holding court for visiting writers, and *The Double Dealer* crowd drew writers to town, publishing the first works of Faulkner and Hemingway. Faulkner's time here inspired his first two novels, *Soldier's Pay* and *Mosquitoes.*

In the 1930s, the WPA project got underway under the leadership of the great and generous Lyle Saxon, and writers came and worked here, discovering even more about the city. *The WPA City Guide to New Orleans* is still being reprinted.

In the twentieth century, many New Orleans writers received critical acclaim. Pulitzer Prize winners included Shirley Ann Grau for *Keepers of the House,* John Kennedy Toole for *A Confederacy of Dunces,* Richard Ford for *Independence Day,* and Robert Olen Butler for *A Good Scent from a Strange Mountain,* a moving collection of stories about Vietnamese immigrants in eastern New Orleans.

Born in Birmingham, Alabama, and a longtime resident of Covington, Louisiana, Walker Percy (1916-1990) was a novelist influenced by Southern sensibilities, Existentialism, and Roman Catholicism who is best known for his 1961 novel The Moviegoer, *for which he won a National Book Award for Fiction. (Photograph © by John R. Kemp, circa 1981.)*

Brenda Marie Osbey received the American Book Award for *All Saints: New and Selected Poems.*

New Orleans also produced a significant number of writers who established reputations as public intellectuals or achieved success as journalists, in addition to producing bestselling books. Among that number, count John Barry, Jason Berry, Andrei Codrescu, Walter Isaacson, Nicholas Lemann, Michael Lewis, and Cokie Roberts. Lively political commentators James Carville and Donna Brazile are also spokespeople for the city.

John Barry's *Rising Tide: The Great Mississippi Flood of 1927 and How It Changed America* achieved bestseller status twice, once upon publication and again post-Katrina. Jason Berry established a reputation for covering the sex abuse scandal in the Catholic church, as well as for his many works about local music and culture. Andrei Codrescu was known for his NPR commentary, collected in several anthologies, as well as his poetry, fiction, and memoir. After a distinguished career at *Time,* Walter Isaacson became a celebrity in his own right as a biographer of such figures as Benjamin Franklin, Albert Einstein, Henry Kissinger, and Steve Jobs. Nicholas Lemann, former dean of the Columbia School of Journalism, writes for the *New Yorker* and is perhaps best known for *The Promised Land: The Great Black Migration and How It Changed America.* Michael Lewis cast a keen eye on financial markets and social change in his books, many of which have been adapted into film—*The Blind*

Grace King (1852-1932) was an acclaimed New Orleans novelist and historian who wrote about the early settlement of Louisiana and nineteenth century Creole culture in New Orleans. (May 1887, courtesy of The Historic New Orleans Collection)

George Washington Cable's best-known novel is The Grandissimes *(1880), which depicted Creole life in nineteenth-century New Orleans. (Courtesy of Peggy Scott Laborde)*

Lafcadio Hearn (1850-1904) was an international writer known especially for his writings about Japan. While residing in New Orleans in the 1870s and 1880s, he wrote extensively and colorfully about the city's Creole culture, Voodoo, crime, demimonde characters, and places. In 1890, he moved to Japan and taught and wrote about Japanese life. (Courtesy of The Historic New Orleans Collection.)

Lyle Saxon (1891-1946) was a New Orleans journalist and historian best known for his books Fabulous New Orleans *and* Gumbo Ya-Ya. *A prominent member of writers and artists who congregated in the New Orleans French Quarter during the 1930s and '40s, Saxon directed the Great Depression-era Federal Writers' Project in Louisiana and* WPA Guide to Louisiana. (Photoprint circa 1930. Gift of Ms. Gretchen Crager Sharpless. Courtesy of The Historic New Orleans Collection.)

Side, The Big Short, and *Moneyball.* Cokie Roberts drew a loyal following for her works of women's history, especially *Capital Dames, Founding Mothers*, and *We Are Our Mothers' Daughters.* Other important voices post-Katrina included Tulane historian Lawrence N. Powell and Tulane geographer Richard Campanella.

One of the great underpinnings of literary culture in New Orleans is its strong tradition of independent bookstores. Faulkner House Books opened in 1990 in the very heart of the Quarter, both a literary landmark and a destination store. The Catholic Bookstore is more than seventy-five years old, serving the nearby Catholic seminary and New Orleans' large Catholic population. Community Book Center has been serving the black community for more than thirty years. Faubourg Marigny Art and Books (FAB) is one of the oldest LGBT bookstores in the country. Uptown neighborhoods have such long-lived stores as Garden District Book Shop and Octavia Books (the over-half-a-century-old Maple Street Book Shop closed in 2017). Mid-City has Tubby and Coo's Mid-City Book Shop and the Broad Street neighborhood has Kitchen Witch, all of which support local authors by hosting events and carrying their books. Crescent City Books is an antiquarian stalwart in the central business district, just as Acadia Books and Beckham's are French Quarter favorites. It takes a lot of bookstores to keep up with New Orleans titles; Amazon lists more than 83,000.

The late twentieth century also saw the rise of an important feature in the cultural landscape—the literary festival. Music and culinary festivals have long been a part of life here, but New Orleans added its special flair to literary festivals, as well—mix booze and parties with larger-than-life personalities and what results? Wonderful stories.

The Tennessee Williams/New Orleans Literary Festival made its debut in 1987, followed by Words and Music: A Literary Feast in New Orleans in 1990, sponsored by the Pirate's Alley Faulkner Society. Both of these events drew large and loyal audiences and provided the important function of showcasing talented local writers, as well as bringing in nationally known authors and editors and agents. The Williams Festival's signature event is the Stanley and Stella Shouting Contest, which invites the public to re-enact that iconic scene of Marlon Brando's anguished cry at the end of *A Streetcar Named Desire.* (In typical New Orleans fashion, there are a fair number of women who yell for Stanley.)

A children's literary festival begun by then-New Orleans First Lady Cheryl Landrieu and Ruby Bridges morphed into the New Orleans Book Festival. The NOLA Book Fair, dedicated to small-press books, takes place every fall. And a newcomer, the New Orleans Poetry Festival, joined the roster in 2016. Despite a fluctuating economy, these festivals have endured, partly because of the tenacity of their founders, partly because any writer not already working in New Orleans wants to come and visit.

After 2005, the very future of New Orleans may have seemed uncertain, but one thing was clear from the very beginning: there would be Katrina books— and lots of them! Beginning with *Why New Orleans Matters* by Tom Piazza, there was a new wave of exploration, justification, and historical interpretation. Katrina did a remarkable thing in that it gave our city a shared story—a narrative of past, present, and future—but it gave each individual a story, as well. Stories became our social currency, collected in archives and anthologies; now, Amazon lists more than 9,000 Katrina titles, including *Breach of Faith: The Life and Near Death of a Great American City,* Douglas Brinkley's *The Great Deluge: Hurricane Katrina, New Orleans, and the Mississippi Gulf Coast,* Ivor Van Heerden's *The Storm: What Went Wrong and Why During Hurricane Katrina—The Inside Story*

The Stanley and Stella Shouting Contest, organized by the Tennessee Williams/New Orleans Literary Festival each year, is the finale to the almost five-day tribute to Williams and the city's rich literary heritage. (Photo by Peggy Scott Laborde)

from One Louisiana Scientist, and John McQuaid and Mark Schleifstein's *Path of Destruction: The Devastation of New Orleans and the Coming Age of Superstorms*.

A new wave of writers came to town post-Katrina, young people who had become interested in the city's unfolding story and wanted to take part in it. James Carville and Mary Matalin made a permanent home in New Orleans with their family. Other recent arrivals include Jami Attenberg, Bret Martin, Nathaniel Rich, and Katy Simpson Smith.

New Orleans boasts a number of contemporary crime novelists, including Laura Lippman (who lives here part-time) and Bill Loehfelm, whose Maureen Coughlin novels are a fascinating inside look at police work, and Nevada Barr, the author of the Anna Pigeon series. New Orleans has always had a robust crime-writing community, which includes such well-known writers as Julie Smith and Christine Wiltz. And the city is home to writers of international reputation: Joseph Boyden from Canada, Yuri Herrera from Mexico, and Niyi Osundare from Nigeria.

In the post-Katrina years, cooperative efforts have enhanced the literary scene. The Antenna Gallery, Room 220, and Press Street have offered impressive literary programming. Groups such as the NOLAFugees, the MelaNated Writers collective, and the Peauxdunque Writers Alliance came into being. New reading series—Dogfish, Blood Jet, the 1718 Reading Series—now exist along with that old standby, the Maple Leaf Bar Sunday afternoon readings, the longest running poetry series in the South.

Some of the great charms and strengths of the city's literary history are its enduring infrastructure, its visibility, and its easy access. It is difficult for a New Orleanian to escape the city's literary history—it's built into every phase of life here, from nursery school parties at Storyland in City Park to field trips to the French Quarter.

Carnival brings parades that often center on themes from books—pageants of stories rolling down the city streets, larger than life. Revelers also sport costumes inspired by books, an homage to beloved characters. Halloween belongs to the Vampire Lestat Fan Club, with balls and elaborate costumes. Thanks to Anne Rice, New Orleans is now one of the top destinations for the October holiday.

Best of all, many of the places where writers lived and worked have been preserved and cherished. A walking tour through the Quarter inevitably includes a stop at Faulkner House, a reverent pause outside the various residences of Tennessee Williams, or a drink at the Hotel Monteleone's Carousel Bar, always a popular watering hole for literati. The Monteleone has also welcomed Truman Capote, William Faulkner, Richard Ford, Eudora Welty, Tennessee Williams, and countless others. There are almost always a few tourists at the corner of First and Chestnut in the Garden District, paying their respects at the former home of Anne Rice, who now lives in California. You can walk in the footsteps of writers you most admire.

Finally, another great literary landmark is the National World War II

Stephen E. Ambrose (right) was an American historian and biographer of US presidents Dwight D. Eisenhower and Richard Nixon. For many years he was a professor of history at the University of New Orleans and the author of numerous bestselling volumes of American popular history. He was a founder of the New Orleans-based National World War II Museum and is shown here with Gordon "Nick" Mueller, the former president and chief executive officer of the museum. The photo was taken on opening day of the museum, June 6, 2000. (Courtesy of the National World War II Museum)

Museum, originally the vision of University of New Orleans historian Stephen Ambrose, who dreamed of honoring the veterans who had shared their oral histories with him for such bestselling books as *Band of Brothers* and *D-Day: June 6, 1944.*

In my work as a literary journalist over the past decades, one thing has happened over and over again. It's just a moment, really. A writer looks across a table and says, "And then I got to New Orleans, and I became myself."

What makes that self-realization possible? What does New Orleans offer? First is a long history, a literary tradition to test one's self against, a culture to absorb, clichés to avoid. Then there is the rich, visual, up close and personal shock of everyday life—rare indeed is the walk in New Orleans that doesn't combine a deep awareness of beauty with a startling moment of ugly reality. For the writer, there are welcoming, extensive libraries and archives, back to full strength now after the devastation of 2005. Most of all, there is the sense that anything is possible.

And what makes literary life here continue? Strong creative writing offerings at the University of New Orleans, Tulane, Loyola, and the New Orleans Center for Creative Arts are producing a new generation. Small publishers abound, as well as Pelican Publishing, which is devoted to books of local interest, cookbooks, and children's books. A new wave of book and paper artists has arrived. Centuries from now, someone will be writing words like mine on whatever electronic device is to come, and New Orleans may have finally become Atlantis, but writers will still be finding inspiration in its very existence.

Susan Larson is the host of The Reading Life *on WWNO, New Orleans' NPR affiliate; she is the author of* The Booklover's Guide to New Orleans, *which has appeared in two editions. From 1988 to 2009, she was the book editor for the* Times-Picayune.

The French Opera House, 1859-1919, provided employment to musicians who also taught music. Some early jazz musicians had family members who played there. (Courtesy of The Historic New Orleans Collection)

Rhythm of a City

Connie Zeanah Atkinson

Almost from its beginning, the city of New Orleans has been associated with music and dancing. Early in its colonial years, locals of all conditions could hear music in a variety of settings—sacred and secular, classical and popular, out of doors and in concert halls. Young New Orleanians took up music, and it became the family business for many who were denied other opportunities. The sheer number of musicians and places to play defined and refined the city's reputation and relationship with the rest of the country and the world.

The city's enthusiasm for music evolved as a practical response of a new people in the new world. In contrast to its Protestant neighbors, Catholic New Orleans had no censure against dance, and for an immigrant destination with people of many languages, dancing was a convenient, inexpensive, and enjoyable means of socializing. Unlike the Puritan founding fathers, people from the African nations, France, and Spain all danced. Locals had an appetite for new dances, and in this busy port, with ships coming in daily from the Caribbean and Gulf, new sounds came ashore with the new arrivals. Musical genealogists trace these rhythms into the city and into the repertoire of local musicians, where styles and beats were absorbed, altered, and incorporated, becoming local signatures, recognizable signs that reaffirmed a local identity, creating community of the disparate and polyglot population of this far-flung place. Simply put, music helped create New Orleans in the local imagination, and the constant need for a musical accompaniment to the city's myriad celebrations created new opportunities for musicians to play.

Although slavery was as violent and abusive in French and Spanish New Orleans as in other places in the South, both French and Spanish colonial governments did allow New Orleanians of African descent some freedom to perform their music, making New Orleans one of the few places in the US where people of European descent could hear and absorb the musical values of the African continent and Afro-Caribbean. In addition, since enslaved New Orleanians had opportunities to make money and thus could attend European-style musical performances, New Orleanians of African descent could absorb European musical values. So from the earliest days, New Orleans was a place where a musician had access to a range of music, and the style of music played was not limited by the musician's ethnicity.

It should come as no surprise, therefore, that in this place the musicians eventually devised a musical style that took advantage of all these varied influences, allowing each musician a voice for his or her own distinct message and the confidence to jump from the written score. And that's what some call America's original art form: jazz. Ah, the irony—a music for, but certainly not of, America's Protestant/Puritan founders became what Albert Murray called "the national soundtrack."

In fact, Wynton Marsalis and others have called jazz a metaphor for democracy— the balance of the individual with the communal. Maybe this explains why the place where this music emerged looms so large in the American imagination—the land of dreamy dreams. Jazz reflected its hometown, an American place with an impulse for diversity, for all to have a voice, a goal seldom reached but a persistent dream nonetheless, revealed in its music. Within the music lay the potential for freedom for all, and worldwide, people heard and responded to that musical message. Jazz became the logo for an age, the sound of freedom, and New Orleans as its site of emergence became forever associated with the music.

To spotlight a few New Orleans musicians in a survey of the city's music is to leave out a host of others equally worthy of mention. The names most familiar to music fans—Armstrong, Gottschalk, Domino, Bechet, Prima, Fountain, Connick—represent but a handful of the creators and craftsmen of New Orleans music. Innovators, masters of their instruments, protégés, mentors, divas, entertainers, and teachers abound. Branches of family trees are heavy with musicians: Humphreys, Batistes, Barbarins, Marsalises, Nevilles. Sidemen with names familiar only to musical insiders brought New Orleans to the likes of James Brown, Duke Ellington, Ornette Coleman. The work, if not the names, of New Orleans studio musicians are recognized by popular music fans everywhere, not to mention those multitude of New Orleans musicians never or seldom captured on disc who created the thousands of magical nights in smoky clubs, moments of ecstasy at festivals and churches, who again and again made us fall in love with our city and sometimes with each other.

This New Orleans jazz funeral celebrated the life of beloved trumpet player DeDe Pierce on November 26, 1973. Note the local dishes offered at the bar/restaurant in the background, including Ya Ca Mein, a type of Asian beef noodle soup known as a cure for hangovers. (Photograph by Justin Winston)

New Orleans clarinet and jazz great Pete Fountain (1930-2016). Born Pierre Dewey LaFontaine, Pete Fountain was celebrated worldwide for his unique style and renditions of New Orleans jazz. (Photo by Armand "Sheik" Richardson, © 2001)

Jazz clarinetist Tim Laughlin continues in the traditional jazz tradition of his mentor, Pete Fountain. This photo was taken at Fountain's funeral in 2016. (Photo by Peggy Scott Laborde)

What links these disparate musicians? Most were products of thick, overlapping networks of families, neighborhoods, and social institutions. Most as children and before formal instruction had heard a variety of music in a variety of places. Many benefitted from a series of mentors and music teachers in and out of the band room willing to share experiences and bandstands with younger musicians. For generations, the pedagogical strategies of New Orleans—long, slow exposure without overpraising, hands-on experience, and opportunities for youngsters—successfully produced generations of excellent and versatile musicians.

Somewhere at the end of the nineteenth century, New Orleans musicians, a little bored with ragtime, began collectively improvising with a mélange of current music: brass band marches, quadrilles, danza, and danzon. From practically the moment of release of the first jazz record by the Original Dixieland Jazz Band in 1917, jazz became the nation's hottest popular music, and the New Orleans jazz musician became the city's big export. The most renowned of these was Louis Armstrong, probably the musician most associated with jazz and with New Orleans. His career mirrored that of many young local musicians—exposure to a variety of musical styles from blues to opera, instruction and mentorship by such as Peter Davis and Joe "King" Oliver—but his virtuosity and innovation, his personal charm and generosity made "Pops" one of the most famous people on earth.

In the 1950s and '60s, New Orleans music again hit big in the recording world, only this time, the recording was done in New Orleans. Some of the best-loved American popular music came out of this period from small, locally owned recording studios. The war years had brought a ban on recordings, and now, tired of war and with money in their pockets from war production jobs, young Americans were ready for new sounds. New Orleans R&B reflected the optimism and youth of the era—simple, fun songs played by master musicians for teenagers to dance to. It was non-threatening, happy music, most exemplified by the artist whose brother-in-law called him a country and western musician,

Fate Marable, on piano, was in charge of music for the Streckfus Steamship Lines. The ships are credited with spreading jazz up and down the Mississippi during the 1920s. Note a very young Louis Armstrong third from right. (Courtesy of the Hogan Jazz Archive/Tulane University)

Antoine "Fats" Domino. Selling more than 100 million records to fans all over the country and across oceans, Domino reflected the idealized worldview of New Orleans: happy, carefree, uncomplicated. Along with Domino were dozens of local recording artists cranking out the hits for jukeboxes from coast to coast. In Cosimo Matassa's J&M studio and later in Allen Toussaint and Marshall Sehorn's SeaSaint studios, the hits just kept on coming, filling the *Billboard* charts and rocking the car radios of the rock 'n' roll years.

Meanwhile, in 1973, the Orleans Parish School Board, with the support of the Arts Council, opened the New Orleans Center for Creative Arts, a tuition-free instruction center for the city's young talent. Although the school's goal was not to produce superstar musicians but rather to furnish an arts education to the city's children, produce them it did, with its first few graduating classes including Harry Connick Jr., Branford Marsalis, Terence Blanchard, Donald Harrison, and Wynton Marsalis. By 1990, Wynton graced the cover of *Time* magazine, which proclaimed "The New Jazz Age." He embraced, unashamedly, the New Orleans music tradition of respect for the past along with personal expression in the present; brushed off New York critics with a disdain to which they were not accustomed; and, as a winner of the Pulitzer Prize and artistic director of New York's Jazz at Lincoln Center, established himself as a jazz icon. His thoughtful reflections on New Orleans jazz history have kept the city of New Orleans in the conversation while his virtuosity has reinforced ideas of New Orleans musicianship.

New Orleans may be primarily known outside the city for jazz, but it is also home to a large gospel community. The birthplace of the Queen of Gospel, Mahalia Jackson, New Orleans was one of the first places where gospel was performed within Catholic churches. Today, music clubs, festivals, and even conventions regularly feature gospel choirs. Writings on New Orleans music often overlook gospel and in doing so miss a major force in the sustaining of musical instruction and performance that support the city's music industry. Also, the emphasis by scholars on jazz and R&B in New Orleans often denies the participation of women, who, for example, are active in gospel in all phases, including organization and administration.

Brass bands, popular in New Orleans since the early nineteenth century, had begun to fade in the city by the 1970s, but an intervention by banjoist/guitarist Danny Barker led to a rebirth of the brass band tradition. Recently returned from a successful career in New York, Barker founded a brass band for the young people of the Fairview Baptist Church. The Fairview Band launched the careers of many young musicians and popular brass bands such as the Dirty Dozen. Through his mentorship and inspiration, today brass bands are synonymous with New Orleans music and culture.

In the 1990s, New Orleans rappers developed their own up-tempo, bass-heavy, call-and-response version of the genre, called bounce music. Around the new millennium, local rappers achieved tremendous success that made many of them multimillionaires, and hip-hop became the city's most lucrative cultural export, mainly because New Orleans was home to two giants of the hip-hop industry, Master P's No Limit Records and the Williams brothers' Cash Money Records. These labels spawned an incredible number of international rap stars. Embracing New Orleans musical traditions, New Orleans rappers incorporate brass band street-parade instrumentations/rhythms and Mardi Gras Indian chants into the hip-hop collage while becoming a prime vehicle for social and political commentary and community celebration.

Two major forces serve as bookends for the story of New Orleans music in this last century: the emergence of jazz and the series of governmental and

Banjo/guitar player Danny Barker was also a jazz historian. Here he is shown leading a second line at the New Orleans Jazz and Heritage Festival in 1974. (Photo by Michael P. Smith, courtesy of The Historic New Orleans Collection)

Born in Ponchatoula, Louisiana, "Soul Queen of New Orleans" Irma Thomas performed at the 1975 New Orleans Jazz and Heritage Festival with the Professionals. (Photograph by Michael P. Smith. Courtesy of The Historic New Orleans Collection.)

Allen Toussaint (1938-2015) was a musician, composer, arranger, and record producer who wrote many of the most popular New Orleans rhythm and blues songs during the 1950s and '60s. This Grammy Award winner had an active performing and recording career. (Photo by Peggy Scott Laborde)

Dr. Michael White and Gregg Stafford have contributed much to the traditional New Orleans jazz scene. They are shown at the Economy Hall Stage at the New Orleans Jazz and Heritage Festival. (Photo by Peggy Scott Laborde)

"Deacon John" Moore has been performing since the 1950s and is included on many classic New Orleans rhythm and blues recordings. (Photo by Peggy Scott Laborde)

Trumpeter Kermit Ruffins is one of the city's most beloved musicians. He leads a band called the Barbecue Swingers. Ruffins is known for cooking barbecue at some of his performances. (Photo by Ian McNulty)

ecological failures that became known as the Katrina event. Neither happened like the events that they were portrayed as—jazz as a cataclysmic event versus jazz as a practical response to myriad influences; Katrina as a cataclysmic hurricane versus Katrina as the culmination of geographic, infrastructural, and social neglect. But those two events shaped the perception of music in New Orleans just as the flooding shaped the topology of the city.

New Orleans post-Katrina remains a city in recovery. Historically drawing its cultural vitality from its non-professional cultural industries—the local celebrations, the street parades, the social institutions—it still suffers the loss of neighborhoods and the dispersal of performers. But despite disruption and disaster, with little support for education and infrastructure, New Orleanians still put their energies into music and the world continues to listen.

Jazz and gospel, R&B and hip-hop, brass bands and rock 'n' roll—the families, neighborhoods, churches, and schools have nurtured and created opportunities for young New Orleanians to find their expression through music. Each generation has used music to express its own distinctive voice while often giving a nod to those who came before. The sounds coming from the wards and neighborhoods may differ, drawn from the distinct history and experience of the residents, but they all thrive under the second-line umbrella of New Orleans music.

Connie Zeanah Atkinson is codirector of the Midlo Center for New Orleans Studies at the University of New Orleans, where for over twenty years she has taught the history of New Orleans music. Atkinson received her PhD from the Institute of Popular Music, Liverpool, England. She worked at the Courier *and* Figaro *newspapers and* New Orleans Magazine *and was editor and publisher of* Wavelength New Orleans Music Magazine.

Pictured inside the New Orleans Item *sports department are Joe Englert (seated in rear), Hap Glaudi, and Ike Morales. Glaudi went on to a successful career as sports director at WWL-TV and later a sports talk-show host on WWL Radio.* (Photo courtesy Phil Johnson)

Members of the WWL-TV news staff are shown in this 1981 photo. (Courtesy of WWL-TV)

Bylines and Busy Times

Dominic Massa

They are the names that brought New Orleanians the news. Names like Scoop, Pie, Iris, Nash, Hap, and even By HEK. One of them, called Podine, had a moniker so memorable that ventriloquist Edgar Bergen named one of his dummies after her. Two others, Garland and Angela, fell in love, married, and divorced, all while anchoring the city's top-rated TV newscast for over a decade. They are all journalists who chronicled the city's modern history while pioneering technology and techniques that people still talk about nationwide.

At the time of the city's two hundred fiftieth anniversary in 1968, there were two daily newspapers (the morning *Times-Picayune* and afternoon *States-Item*). While three television stations (Channels 4, 6, and 12) produced newscasts, some of them were still only fifteen minutes long. Radio, a fixture in the city since 1922, remained a source of news, but most listeners turned to it for music or talk, just like today. The *Vieux Carré Courier*, established seven years earlier, was an important voice in the alternative press, but *Figaro* and *Gambit* were still a decade or so away. *New Orleans Magazine* was in its infancy. The *Louisiana Weekly* had been around for forty years, but only a handful of blacks worked in local media. The internet was nonexistent.

Now, as the city marks its three hundredth birthday, websites and social media are redefining how local news is produced and consumed. There are two papers again, but one (the *Times-Picayune*/NOLA.com) embraces a digital strategy while the other (the *New Orleans Advocate*) prints and delivers papers seven days a week. Television stations produce several hours of newscasts each day on a schedule that begins at the once-unimaginable hour of 4:30 a.m. Women and blacks hold high-ranking positions in newsrooms. Local journalists are tech-savvy, bright, and energetic. Still, not one of them has a Ninth Ward seafood joint named after him. That would be fabled *States-Item* police reporter Richard "Jack" Dempsey. Maybe that's why he signed every story he wrote "ALIHOT"—"a legend in his own time."

Besides Dempsey, two other legends are also better known by their nicknames—Lloyd "Hap" Glaudi and Bernard "Buddy D" Diliberto. Both were cut from the same blue-collar cloth, with New Orleans accents to match. Glaudi wrote for the *Item* for twenty-five years before making a leap to WWL-TV, where his colorful sportscasts (which always included Fair Grounds race results) endeared him to a generation of fans. Diliberto began at the *Times-Picayune* before finding even greater fame on television and radio (at WVUE, WDSU, and WWL Radio) despite a speech impediment and mastery of malapropism.

Terry Flettrich was one of the first women on television in New Orleans, producing test programs for WDSU before it signed on the air in 1948. She is best known as host of Midday *on WDSU from the 1950s through the 1970s. (Photo courtesy Terry Flettrich Rohe)*

Both sportscasters were educated by the Jesuits, and Jesuit-run Loyola University owned and operated WWL Radio and WWL-TV, which signed on in 1957. Loyola sold both stations in the late 1980s after developing them into market leaders that earned national accolades. Much of the credit for that success is given to J. Michael Early, the labor lawyer turned-general manager who ran both operations for more than three decades. Early was essentially following a formula set by WDSU, the state's first television station. Channel 6 began broadcasting on December 18, 1948. At the time, television was still seen by many as a fad. For the well-known Stern family, who owned the station, it was partly a way to find their son Edgar Jr., a job. As the medium developed, Channel 6 became a national leader in terms of programming and news coverage. Station managers Robert Swezey and A. Louis Read and program director Jerry Romig turned WDSU's home base—inside the historic Seignouret-Brulatour mansion at 520 Royal Street—into a headquarters for quality broadcasting.

Many of WDSU's early stars came to television from radio, including sports director Mel Leavitt, who is also fondly remembered for his Carnival coverage. Another pioneer, Terry Flettrich Rohe, became best-known as children's show host Mrs. Muffin and as the producer and host of *Midday*, a popular local version of NBC's *Today*. Its stable of stars included TV icons Wayne Mack and Bob and Jan Carr, entertainment critic Al Shea, weather guru Nash Roberts, and newsmen Alec Gifford and Ed Planer.

Terry Flettrich welcomes children to the set of her popular Mrs. Muffin show on WDSU in the 1950s. (Courtesy Terry Flettrich Rohe)

Planer also wrote and delivered nightly editorials, a practice started by WDSU on September 15, 1958—just as the *New Orleans Item* newspaper ceased publication. Its demise meant a media monopoly for the city's two surviving newspapers (both of whom shared an owner) and also meant the city had one fewer editorial voice. Early on, WDSU took a strong stance in favor of school desegregation, which angered some viewers but won the station a 1959 George Foster Peabody award. News director Bill Monroe (who later went to NBC News as host of *Meet the Press)* was the station's first editorial voice. Later, editorials by Planer and news director John Corporon were credited with helping to kill the proposed Riverfront Expressway. WDSU can also claim the first TV editorial cartoonist. John Chase, who had made a name for himself in the city's newspapers, drew and narrated editorial cartoons nightly on Channel 6 throughout the 1960s. When it launched its own daily editorial in 1962, WWL-TV found a bearded bard for the job. Phil Johnson was a former *Item* newsman who later became the station's news director. He would deliver editorials on Channel 4 until 1999 while also producing documentaries that earned the station three of its seven Peabody awards.

When WDSU was sold to out-of-town owners in 1972, Johnson and Early seized the opportunity to expand WWL's news operation and climb to the top of the local ratings. The list of television greats they cultivated for Channel 4's staff includes Bill Elder, Jim Metcalf, Angela Hill, Garland Robinette, Jim

This photo shows the city room of the New Orleans Item *shortly before it closed in 1958. The afternoon newspaper was in operation from 1924 until it merged with the New Orleans States in 1958. In 1962, both papers were then purchased by the* Times-Picayune. *(Courtesy of Phil Johnson)*

Phil Johnson is shown here without his familiar beard, soon after delivering his first WWL-TV editorial in 1962. In addition to delivering editorials for thirty-seven years, Johnson was also Channel 4's news director, assistant general manager, and award-winning documentary producer. (Courtesy of WWL-TV)

Members of WDSU-TV's 1960s stable of stars are featured in this promotional photograph. From left to right are Alec Gifford, Bill Slatter, Mel Leavitt, Terry Flettrich, John Chase, Nash Roberts, Jan Carr, Bob Carr, and Wayne Mack. (Photo courtesy Bob and Jan Carr)

Henderson, Dennis Woltering, Norman Robinson, Eric Paulsen, Sally-Ann Roberts, Bill Capo, Meg Farris, and Frank Davis. Add to that competitors such as investigative ace Richard Angelico; weather whizzes Bob Breck and Margaret Orr; reporters Bill Rouselle and Furnell Chatman (the city's first black TV reporters); and pioneering photojournalists Del Hall, Mike Lala, M. J. Gauthier, Jim Tolhurst, and Willie Wilson, and you see why for local TV viewers, the memories remain vivid, even if some of what they saw was in black and white.

The well-known names of New Orleans news are by no means limited to broadcasting. Two titans of print journalism were women, better known by pen names. One wrote essays and poems as Pearl Rivers. In real life, she was Eliza Jane Poitevent Holbrook Nicholson. She married the owner of the *Picayune,* and when he died in 1876, she became America's first female newspaper publisher. In 1896, Elizabeth Gilmer began writing an advice column as Dorothy Dix. It would later be syndicated in newspapers worldwide. Two other pioneering female journalists, Iris Kelso and Rosemary James, covered local politics for decades. Kelso, a "steel magnolia" with the southern drawl to match, was a reporter and columnist for the *States-Item* and the *Times-Picayune.* At the *States-Item,* James, along with Dempsey and reporter Dave Snyder, broke the news that District Attorney Jim Garrison was investigating the Kennedy assassination.

Columnists have always been among local papers' more colorful personalities. That includes Charles "Pie" Dufour, whose nickname gave his column the perfect title: "Pie's à la Mode." In more than 9,700 columns (always written on a manual typewriter), Dufour covered a wide range of topics, from Toscanini

Angela Hill came to New Orleans in 1975 for a job at WWL-TV as consumer reporter. During her thirty-eight-year career there, she went on to become one of the city's best-known and most-beloved news anchors. (Courtesy of WWL-TV)

and Tulane football to the Civil War and Carnival. Kings and queens appear regularly in the columns of Nell Nolan, who has spent nearly forty years chronicling New Orleans' social scene. Betty Guillaud covered the comings and goings of New Orleans' society and celebrities for decades while also popularizing the "Big Easy" nickname for the city. Outdoors columnist Harry Elliott Klein (whose byline was By HEK) earned loyal readers, as did feature columnists Angus Lind, Frank Schneider, Ronnie Virgets, and Chris Rose. Critics Frank Gagnard, David Cuthbert, Mark Lorando, Richard Collin, and Gene Bourg held forth on dining, entertainment, and TV in sections often supplemented by the work of Millie Ball (travel and other features) and Susan Larson (books). Sports columnist Peter Finney's career spanned an unbelievable seventy years. He went to work for the *States-Item* in 1945 as a Loyola freshman. He would join the *Times-Picayune* in 1980 and remain a regular on its sports page until 2013.

Finney's byline, like those of reporters Walt Philbin, Bruce Eggler, Susan Finch, John Pope, and many others, appeared in more than one of the city's papers over the years as the publications' names took on hyphenated additions through mergers. For six years in the 1980s, the result was a mouthful: the *Times-Picayune/States-Item*. That paper traced its roots to the *Picayune*, which began publication in 1837. It merged with the *Times-Democrat* and then in 1914 became the *Times-Picayune*. We bring up the lineage to cite another of the important names in local journalism: Phelps. Ashton Phelps was president of the new combined newspaper. His son Esmond, grandson Ashton Sr., and great-grandson Ashton Phelps Jr. continued in the role of publisher for close

Peter Finney chronicled the New Orleans sports scene for sixty-eight years as a reporter and columnist for the New Orleans States, *the* States-Item, *and the* Times-Picayune. *(Photo courtesy of NOLA Media Group/the* Times-Picayune*)*

to 100 years. In 1962, the paper was sold to Advance Publications, owned by Samuel I. Newhouse of New York. Under new owners, the *Times-Picayune* and *States-Item* moved their operations to a new facility at 3800 Howard Avenue.

If New Orleanians didn't know the Newhouse name then, they would learn it in 2012, with news that would rock the local media landscape. Just after celebrating its 175th anniversary, the *Times-Picayune* announced a plan to cut home delivery to three days a week, leaving New Orleans as one of the few major US cities without a daily newspaper. The owners cited higher printing costs, lower ad revenues, and declining readership as reasons to shift focus to the website, NOLA.com. A new company, NOLA Media Group, would accompany the change, which also meant the loss of some 200 jobs. "Our news organization has decided not to sit idly by as passive witnesses to our own decline," longtime editor Jim Amoss wrote in a piece defending the changes. He recounted the paper's stellar coverage of Hurricane Katrina, which earned the paper and its staff (including veteran reporters Mark Schleifstein, Bruce Nolan, and Frank Donze) two Pulitzer Prizes. Amoss explained that many readers followed the coverage on a computer screen and not a printed page. "I didn't realize at that moment that I was witnessing the beginning of our part of the revolution that is transforming our business," Amoss wrote.

The transformation was underway, but it was met with strong public outcry and passionate efforts to find another local owner for the paper (maybe even Saints owner Tom Benson, some hoped). Advance Publications owner Steven Newhouse infamously told the *New York Times,* "We have no intention of selling, no matter how much noise there is out there." That did little to quell the "noise." If anything, it pushed the Baton Rouge-based *Advocate* to expand its local coverage and offer daily home delivery in the area, only to be purchased the next year by billionaire businessman John Georges. In the ensuing months, Georges beefed up the paper by hiring many *Picayune* veterans, including editors Peter Kovacs, Dan Shea, and Martha Carr; columnists James Gill and Stephanie Grace; investigative editor Gordon Russell; music writer Keith Spera; cartoonist Walt Handelsman; and others.

As the news business grapples with change, many would say competition has made it stronger. The newspapers and TV stations battle for readers and viewers (online, on air, and in print). Station-newspaper partnerships, once unheard of, are now the norm. WWL and the *Advocate* regularly share content, while WVUE-TV (owned from 2008 to 2017 by Tom Benson) won a Peabody award for an investigative series coproduced with NOLA.com.

While many of the names and faces may have changed over the years, the success stories in local journalism are still about longevity, personality, and originality. Terry Flettrich Rohe, who had all three traits, reflected: "We really had to crawl into whatever ingenuity, intuitiveness or imagination we had. And, you know, I guess it wasn't too bad because as I think about what we did, some of it is about as good as it gets."

Dominic Massa, executive producer at WWL-TV, has authored two books on New Orleans broadcasting history. The winner of a regional Emmy, he has contributed to more than twenty-five cultural/historical documentaries at WYES-TV. He has written for New Orleans Magazine, Gambit, *the* New Orleans Advocate, *and* Arthur Hardy's Mardi Gras Guide. *A past president of the Press Club of New Orleans, Massa is a recipient of the group's top broadcast reporting honor, the Jim Metcalf Memorial Award.*

Shifting Power Center

Robert L. Dupont

In 1968, as New Orleans looked back over the 250 years since its founding, an illuminated sign hung over Gallier Hall to remind the citizens of the anniversary. The historic building was not the seat of government. The building boom of the 1950s had seen the construction of a new civic center on Perdido Street that included the new City Hall. Those 250 years had firmly established the city's reputation as a hotbed of intense, even raucous politics. But nothing in those two and one-half centuries had prepared New Orleanians for the events of the next fifty years. During that latter period, the city experienced a revolution in politics that saw the dissolution of traditional Deep South Democratic politics, the rise of Republican opposition, neighborhood-level activism, and, most important, the emergence of black voters as the dominant force in urban politics. By the time New Orleanians would celebrate the city's three hundredth anniversary, that revolution would produce the city's first black mayor, two father-son holders of the mayor's office, urban politics that echoed national trends, and the post-Katrina trauma of disaster and recovery.

Mayor deLesseps "Chep" Morrison (1912-1964) dedicating the Franklin Avenue Overpass, 1956. Born in New Roads, Louisiana, Morrison was mayor of New Orleans from 1946 to 1961. The unsuccessful three-time candidate for governor is credited for numerous modernization projects in post-World War II New Orleans. From 1961 to 1963, Morrison served as the US ambassador to the Organization of American States. He and his young son died in a plane crash in Mexico. (Photograph by Leon Trice, 1956. Courtesy of The Historic New Orleans Collection.)

The political transformation began with the mayoral election of 1970. The genial, slightly comical, and often underestimated Victor Schiro had been elected to the office in 1961 and 1965, negotiating a precise course between old-time Democratic politics and the reformist tendencies of the Chep Morrison era. Schiro's 1966 campaign tactics took note of the growing black registration and exploited white fears by constant reference to the dangers of the "bloc" vote.

By 1970, black registration had grown even larger, thanks to the federal Voting Rights Act and local activism. The Louisiana Constitution of 1898 had removed black votes as a significant factor in city politics. Now, more than

Victor H. Schiro (1904-1992), who became mayor of New Orleans in 1961 with the resignation of Mayor de Lesseps Morrison, was elected to serve two terms during the tumultuous 1960s. He was known for his calm style and reluctant but pragmatic approach to desegregation during his administration. (Campaign matchbook, 1961. Gift of Mrs. Denvrich Lebreton. Courtesy of The Historic New Orleans Collection.)

Born Maurice Edwin Landrieu in New Orleans, Moon enjoyed an extensive career in Louisiana and New Orleans politics, serving in the Louisiana House of Representatives (1960-1966), on the New Orleans City Council (1966-1970), as New Orleans mayor (1970-1978), as US Secretary of Housing and Urban Development (1979-1981), and on the Louisiana 4th Circuit Court of Appeals (1992-2000). The father of US senator Mary Landrieu and New Orleans Mayor Mitch Landrieu, Moon headed a progressive administration as mayor, opening the social and political arena to the city's African American community. (Photograph by Tipery, courtesy of The Historic New Orleans Collection.)

seventy years later, white candidates for mayor would have to consider a new element in their strategies. The simple dichotomy of establishment versus reform no longer applied. The reformers had been part of the power structure since 1946, and individual loyalties shifted between the two groups. Electoral politics had become more complex, and candidates scrambled to assemble a coalition. New political organizations within the black community discovered the ability to issue demands and set the agenda. In the runoff between Moon Landrieu and Jimmy Fitzmorris, the white electorate split, providing the new enfranchised black voters with the power to decide the outcome. Fitzmorris hedged his bets and did not firmly commit to bring blacks into his administration. Landrieu made the commitment, won the election (with 90 percent of the black vote), and took over the mayor's office in 1970.

The Landrieu administration quickly followed up on the promise of the campaign. Black political support resulted in appointments to city jobs, participation in federal programs, and more traditional forms of political patronage such as government contracts. These developments were new only in the crossing of racial lines. The new mayor's attention to this constituency mimicked the manner in which the political progress had assimilated other groups (e.g., Irish, Germans, and Italians) in years past. The mayor's actions took place within the context of national urban politics and policy. The domestic disturbances of the 1960s combined with postwar urbanization to increase the minority proportion of populations within inner cities. "White flight," the result of resistance to school desegregation and the attraction of new housing, served to divide city and suburb. The process eventually resulted in political shifts as well. The previously dominant Democratic Party in local and state politics gave way to an authentic two-party system.

The drive for civil rights had other impacts on the national scene that affected New Orleans. The Civil Rights Act of 1964 and the Voting Rights Act of 1965 transformed both society and politics. The response of the national Democratic Party—embodied in Great Society legislation—included programs of aid to urban areas and residents. The War on Poverty explicitly identified the goal of participatory politics. The grassroots goal-setting and leadership aims fit with Mayor Landrieu's obligations to the black constituency to whom he owed his election. And federal largesse eased the financial problems of the city at a time when the population began to decline.

The transition of black activists to political organizers and then to political appointees proceeded rapidly. The various organizations crucial to the mobilization of black votes—SOUL, BOLD, COUP, and others—grew in power as they enjoyed the benefits of being inside the system. The mayor appointed blacks to previously all-white boards and commissions, and he entrusted both city departments and federal programs to his new allies. By the end of Landrieu's second term, New Orleans politics looked nothing like its earlier history.

The 1978 mayoral election to succeed Landrieu rivaled the 1970 contest for drama. Black registration continued to grow; by the end of the decade, white voters were only slightly a majority among Democratic voters in Orleans Parish. The election marked the entry of Ernest "Dutch" Morial into the race. In the runoff, he faced conservative Joseph DiRosa, whom many activists feared would return the city to its pre-1960s outlook. In simplistic terms, the electorate broke down to black, conservative white (trending Republican), and "liberal" white voters loyal to the Landrieu policies. This last group played the role that black voters played in 1969—i.e., white liberals would be the pivotal votes in a closely contested race. Morial became the city's first black mayor, a remarkable achievement in a city where only twenty years earlier, white Democrats had outnumbered black Democrats by a five-to-one margin.

Morial's two terms in office were contentious. Though he served as president of the US Conference of Mayors, he struggled to retain political support within the city. A police strike resulted in the cancellation of all Mardi Gras parades in 1979 as the union tested the resolve of the mayor. And in 1984, the Louisiana World Exposition opened to fanfare but quickly ran into financial troubles. Overly optimistic attendance projections formed the basis for a revenue base that never materialized. The mayor viewed the fair organizers as representative of the white business establish-

Ernest "Dutch" Morial was the mayor of New Orleans from 1978-1986. Prior to that, he served in the Louisiana legislature and became an Appeals Court judge. He was the first African American to be elected to each of these positions. (Photo by Peggy Scott Laborde)

ment and was skeptical of the fair's business model. His accurate assessment won him no friends. Ironically, though the fair ended in bankruptcy, it provided lasting contributions to the city's development, especially in the reinvigoration of the riverfront. The Louisiana Pavilion formed the basis of the city's convention center (eventually named in honor of Morial, who died in 1989).

By the time of the 1986 election, black registration surpassed white, though by a slim margin. That gap would grow to a twenty percentage point advantage early in the next century. The white electorate transitioned from dominance to minority status but gained an ability to decide among black candidates. In that process, the distinctive racial composition of New Orleans had great effect. In every election, the white electorate tended to support the "Creole" candidate for mayor. This traditional leadership group (drawn mainly from French, mixed-race, and Catholic backgrounds) could appeal across racial lines more easily than its opponents.

The 1986 winner was Sidney Barthelemy, a genial, ex-seminarian, COUP-based leader who had first entered government under the Landrieu administration as director of the Department of Welfare. He won the mayoral election with less than 50 percent of the black vote but a high proportion of the votes from the white electorate. Barthelemy's administration began under a fiscal cloud and had difficulty recovering. The Reagan years had reduced federal spending on urban problems, the Louisiana economy suffered from lagging oil prices, and the city's population continued to decline from its peak in 1960 (approximately 627,000) to less than 500,000 in 1990. A seemingly intractable spike in robbery and murder rates bedeviled the city administration, though the electorate returned Barthelemy to office for a second term.

Barthelemy presided over the city's increased dependence on tourism and events for economic development. Building on the efforts of the World's Fair, the Aquarium of the Americas, the riverfront streetcar, and the Riverwalk shopping center opened the river to tourists and locals alike. The New Orleans Convention Center began to expand as a venue for large corporate and association meetings. By the end of Barthelemy's two terms, the city population had stabilized and the economy was on the rebound.

In 1994, a strong white candidate, Donald Mintz, challenged the pattern of the previous four elections. After a primary of seven candidates (including Mitch Landrieu, son of Moon Landrieu), the top two candidates were Mintz and Marc Morial, son of the late mayor Dutch Morial. A close runoff resulted in a Morial victory with 54 percent of the vote. He took office at a difficult time, the murder rate the primary issue. Only a few months after his inauguration, the mayor faced substantial corruption within the New Orleans Police Department. He brought in Richard Pennington from Washington, DC, to assist. After a shocking triple murder in 1996, citizen protest and a community policing initiative began to reduce the crime problem.

Marc Morial benefitted from the recovery of the national economy in the 1990s. He continued the city's transition to a tourist-oriented economic base, including expansion to the convention center and negotiations that brought the NBA back to New Orleans. He enjoyed strong favorability ratings for most of his two terms but also suffered from a public perception that he overemphasized political patronage. As his father before him, he attempted to change the city charter to remove the two-term limitation, but voters rejected the effort.

The election of 2002 attracted a large field, including both newcomers and established politicians. The primary promoted two newcomers to the runoff—Police Superintendent Richard Pennington and businessman C. Ray Nagin. Media interests emphasized Nagin's business background as a contrast to Morial's political patronage. Pennington, as a member of the previous administration, carried the baggage of that criticism. Nagin won the election handily, with much of his support coming from white voters. In a heavily Democratic city, Nagin was not a party stalwart. His background in a regulated industry, cable TV, led him to support candidates from both parties. His first few years in office saw increased tourism and the establishment of a strong film industry in the city, thanks mostly to a generous program of state tax credits.

Toward the end of Nagin's first term, Hurricane Katrina hit the city. Some criticized the mayor's response to the disaster; his re-election seemed unlikely. But he turned the 2006 election into a civil rights contest, asserting that New Orleans was "a chocolate city" and should remain so. The controversial remark not only increased racial tensions in the damaged city but also upset Nagin's strong contingent of white supporters from his first election. Mitch Landrieu once again entered the mayoral contest, along with Ron Forman of the Audubon Nature Institute, Rob Couhig (frequent Republican candidate), lawyer Virginia Boulet, and others. A spirited primary election resulted in a runoff between Landrieu and Nagin. Nagin won the runoff with a reversal of the 2002 voting pattern: his white support fell to 20 percent, but his black support increased to 80 percent. Post-election analysis identified a strong white vote for Nagin among conservative Republicans reluctant to vote for a member of the strongly Democratic Landrieu clan.

Observers from all political persuasions viewed Nagin's second term as a series of disappointments, if not disasters. Recovery from the hurricane was slow and the city's efforts to speed the process unsuccessful. Nagin hired Ed Blakely as recovery "czar," an appointment that backfired when Blakely made himself remarkably unpopular with the community. In 2008, the national recession added to the city's woes, though reconstruction funds from governmental and insurance sources mitigated the recession's effects on New Orleans. Nagin's second term ended in 2010, but by that time numerous stories of alleged corruption had appeared in the local press. The federal government indicted Nagin in 2013, charging him with twenty-one counts of corruption. A jury convicted him on twenty counts, and the presiding judge sentenced him to ten years in prison. He was the only mayor in the history of the city to be indicted on such charges.

In the mayoral election of 2010, Mitch Landrieu made his third attempt at the office. In spite of the presence of several other candidates, he won in the primary with over 66 percent of the vote. Landrieu benefitted from his family connections (son of a previous mayor and brother to a US senator) and from "buyer's remorse" on the part of Nagin voters from 2006. In many ways, the city had come full circle from his father's victory in 1970. Mitch Landrieu replicated the multi-racial coalition of his father and emphasized an inclusive city administration. He won again in 2014 in the first primary.

Problems remained, and solutions were elusive. In 2010, the country was slowly emerging from the reces-sion. Tourism in New Orleans had recovered from its Katrina low but had not yet returned to pre-2005 lev-els. Infrastructure remained a particu-

Mayor Mitch Landrieu, son of former mayor Moon Landrieu, is a former state legislator and lieutenant governor. He is seen here at the annual Riverwalk Lundi Gras celebration with Adonis Exposé, King Zulu 2017, and Dr. Stephen Hales, Rex 2017. (Photo by Peggy Scott Laborde)

lar issue as post-Katrina damage worsened projects neglected for years, result-ing in potholes and incessant water leaks. The spike in crime moderated after Landrieu's inauguration but went up temporarily in 2011. The city's fiscal condition continued to be fragile, and the mayor's effort to impose a public safety fee failed at the polls. But the steady increase in tourism and the backlog of Katrina aid to the city sustained the local economy in spite of a continuing downturn in the oil industry. Hotel occupancy increased, cruise ships contrib-uted to the flow of tourists, and the National World War II Museum continued to attract attention as a national and international attraction.

The cycle of politics over the past fifty years solidified the importance of black participation as both voters and candidates; no longer is a significant portion of the population kept from democratic participation. During the half century, six mayors have served—four black and two white. Two father-son sets dominate thirty-two years of that period. The city is much smaller due to white flight, an expanding metropolitan area, and the lingering effects of the 2005 hurricane and flood. Future politics must confront these new realities but will do so in a city that is more diverse and inclusive than the 1960s version of New Orleans.

Robert L. Dupont is Associate Professor of History at the University of New Orleans and chair of the Department of History and Philosophy. He teaches urban history, twentieth-century American history, and the history of post-World War II Europe. He is a lifelong resident of New Orleans and the author of On Higher Ground: The University of New Orleans at 50.

The Right of the People Peaceably to Assemble (and Dance)

Lolis Eric Elie

We dance after funerals.
We dance on Sundays.
We dance on rooftops.
We dance in the streets.
Why don't we dance during civil rights demonstrations?

The question was so ridiculous, so preposterous, that it could only have been asked by a native of a place so primitive that they actually dance during civil rights demonstrations.

And so it was.

Having just finished our tour through the declining glories of the Vieux Carré, we encountered a demonstration. I don't remember the catalyst for the unrest. (Is it just me, or does it not seem that some people are always unrested?) Insufficiently awed by the glories of the T-shirt shops and bars that form our profitable paean to the French occupation, my South African guest had the temerity to ask why the marchers weren't dancing.

It took me a minute to even process the question. How can you convey so basic a concept? *We dance when we are happy. We protest when we are sad. The people protesting are sad.* Before I could utter a word, it occurred to me: My guest was from South Africa, a place where the dancing protests of the people had helped usher democracy into a nation previously innocent of it. *Toyi-toyi*, as they call it, was a dance the Zimbabwe People's Revolutionary Army invented in their struggle against totalitarian rule. South Africans had incorporated it into their freedom struggle, and, with the election of Nelson Mandela, the *toyi-toyi* as tactic had received another modicum of vindication.

So the question wasn't so ridiculous. But it was still foreign, born of a different world from our world here.

Or was it?

Years later, in an apparent effort to worsen the woes visited by the failure of the federal levees, city "leaders" entertained the idea of not redeveloping certain portions of flood-ravaged New Orleans. The populace, both at home and in exile, was therefore rife with well-founded fears that Hurricane Katrina would be the catalyst, the excuse, for a polite plot to de-Africanize New Orleans. In response, a coalition of twenty-seven social aid and pleasure clubs organized a parade on January 15, 2006. Participants wore black T-shirts emblazoned with the words renew orleans. Benefit, Desire, Pleasure, Humanity, their signs proclaimed, and these were not mere platitudes. These were actual street signs bearing the names of vistas in flood-ravaged African-American neighborhoods. Neighborhoods that, if the worst fears were realized, would no longer be inhabited in the future city.

I understood something then: This was not the advent of a new kind of political New Orleans parade. Rather, this was the conscious articulation of resistance that had grown out of a tradition that from its earliest roots was about protest and pleasure and desire and humanity and benefit.

Street parades in New Orleans have a multi-ethnic history. New Orleanians of West African, Haitian, Sicilian, and Irish descent have all paraded. Much of this activity was sponsored by mutual aid societies, organizations that, as early as the 1800s, provided assistance when members were sick, unemployed, or in need of emotional support or a proper New Orleans burial. These groups also sponsored a signature annual parade. These parades have come to be known as second lines, named after the dancers who form a second line of revelers that fall in line after the first line—the hired band and the hiring organization. But, as the Irish and Sicilians "became white," to appropriate the phrase Noel Ignatiev turned to title his book, the parading tradition among them declined precipitously. As African Americans have yet to manage—or been allowed to manage—a similar sleight of hand, the tradition of second line parades remains emblematically strong among black New Orleanians.

Perhaps the black version of this tradition owes its longevity to the fact that it stems from different, deeper stimuli—stimuli that yet abide even in these more genteel times.

In its opening words, Le Code Noir of 1724, the document best known for regulating black-white relations, decrees that all Jews be expelled. With that nasty bit of business settled, the code goes on to the matters of Negroes and Catholicism, the former being required to be instructed in the hypocrisies of the latter and given Sundays off to better accomplish the purpose. No doubt there existed among the populace some who gladly would have exchanged the tedium of work for the boredom of white worship, but many others deemed the pursuit of pleasure more worthy of their time. So excited were they to do their thing that in 1786 Gov. Esteban Miró had to forbid *los tangos, o bailes de negros* (the tango, or dances of the blacks) to be performed before the end of vespers. These black dancers gathered in various places around the enslaved city to socialize until 1817 when a new decree directed that Sunday pleasures had to be centralized in Congo Square, a park on Rampart Street in Faubourg Treme, directly across the street from the Vieux Carré. There the descendants of the Ibo, Bamana, Kongo, and Creoles danced African dances, played African music, cooked African food, and created a marketplace for their produce, dishes, and crafts. In so doing, they worked the roots of the city's emblematic cultural expressions.

I imagine that, had it been allowed, the men and women of Congo Square might well have mobilized themselves, second line fashion, through the streets of the city. But they couldn't. And here we have the meeting of the two themes that define the black parading tradition of New Orleans—the desire of black New Orleans to express itself in its own way and on its own streets and the desire of official New Orleans to regulate how, when, where, and whether such expressions will be allowed. Haunting every parade is the specter of police disrespect or violence.

"Sometimes I think that the antagonism between the police and the second liners is almost part of the tradition," LSU professor Helen Regis said in an interview with historian Ned Sublette in 2006. "Sometimes they seem to almost egg each other on. Sometimes the police use their sirens to push people up the

The Avenue Steppers Marching Club, 1982. View of a large second line parade with the Pin Stripe Brass Band on the street in front of Big Time Crip's, a disabled American veterans bar located at 1939 Second Street in Central City. The Avenue Steppers organized as a marching club in October 1981 and are shown celebrating the "Blessing of the Banner" at their first annual parade, June 6, 1982. (Photograph by Michael P. Smith, 1982. Courtesy of The Historic New Orleans Collection.)

Emile Victor Clay jazz funeral, 1996. Emile Victor Clay was a chef and member of several New Orleans fraternal or benevolent associations, including Young Men Olympia, Knights of Peter Claver, and the Elks Hall. He was seventy-three years old when he died on February 7, 1996. After a mass at Holy Ghost Catholic Church on Louisiana Avenue, the jazz funeral procession marched to Lafayette Cemetery No. 2. (Photograph by Michael P. Smith, 1996. Courtesy of The Historic New Orleans Collection.)

street. Why are they doing that? I don't know, but it makes people mad; it really does. Sometimes the dancers in a second line will start gyrating against the police car in a provocative way that seems designed to make the police mad. So then the police are being challenged to keep their cool and not worry about it."

In his 1961 book, *Treat It Gentle*, the great clarinetist Sidney Bechet recalls the unpredictability of the parade police. "The police would come by sometimes and, like I say, some of them didn't do nothing to stop what was going on, but others used to beat up the people and break them up and get them moving away from there. You'd just never knew which it would be those police."

In their books, *Congo Square: African Roots in New Orleans* and *Congo Square in New Orleans*, Freddi Williams Evans and Jerah Johnson, respectively, chronicle not only the history of the gathering place but also the history of the regulation thereof. "In 1837, the city council authorized 'free negroes and slaves to give balls on the Circus Square [Congo Square] from 12 o'clock until sunset under surveillance of the police,'" Johnson writes. In 1845, the strictures were tightened. Africans were allowed to gather provided they had written permission from their own personal white folks, and the rules limited the dances to the hours between 4:00 and 6:30, limited them to summer months, and had eight policemen stationed as overseers and to made sure that their activities would not be "offensive to public decency." (Left to interpretation was the most relevant question: How could it be possible to offend public decency in a slavocracy?)

Though limited in time, place, and duration, these West African-derived processions are best seen as assertions of ownership of public space. In the exercise of the bones and ligaments of dance is also embodied the exercise of the first civil right articulated in the bill of rights. "A second line is in effect a civil rights demonstration," Ned Sublette said in Jordan Flaherty's 2010 book, *Bloodlines: Community and Resistance From Katrina to the Jena Six*.

Though largely irrelevant for its first two centuries, that bill guarantees by name several of the rights on exercise when Mardi Gras Indians or social aid and pleasure clubs take to the streets: "Congress shall make no law respecting an establishment of religion, or prohibiting the free exercise thereof; or abridging the freedom of speech, or of the press; or the right of the people peaceably to assemble, and to petition the Government for a redress of grievances."

This tradition is a way for me to connect myself physically, mentally, emotionally, spiritually, back to my ancestral homeland—one bead at a time. You tried to sever those ties, but I found a way.
—Queen Cherice Harrison-Nelson, Guardians of the Flame,
from *It's Your Glory: The Big Queens of Carnival*

The purpose is to have fun. To entertain one's self, as it says in our charter. It's basically what the culture is. It's a culture which expresses the joy of life. No matter how miserable and how oppressive life gets, that once a year you can go out with your friends, your relatives, your good friends, you hire a band, you get dressed up, really looking good and the streets are yours. One day a year.
—Joe Stern, Original Prince of Wales Social Aid and Pleasure Club

It was like Christmas. Like a toy. You couldn't wait until Christmas come. It was similar to that. I was born into this culture so I always did love it. This is something that a majority of kids and everybody in the community loved—masquerading. It was exciting, being a Mardi Gras Indian. It was like Indian fever, that's what they call it. When you catch Indian Fever, that's all you breathe. That's all you think.
—Victor Harris, Big Chief of the Mandingo Warriors, Spirit of the Fi Yi Yi,
from *The Big Chiefs of Carnival: Spirit Leads My Needle*

I just love to see the look on everybody's face when we come from wherever we are coming from and they are like, "They're clean. They're pretty." It's like bragging rights. Bragging rights. . . . Why we do it? Because our forefathers couldn't come on Front Street, they had to be on Back Street.

—Angelina Sever, Divine Ladies Social Aid and Pleasure Club

Parading on the street is a beautiful thing, if you're for the right thing. That's the way our club looks at it. And what I call the right thing is not the most expensive pants, shirt, shoes, hats. It's the colors and the spirit you bring out there to show folks that we only want to enjoy our life for these four hours after a hard day of work. You have one day just to like relax, hear some beautiful jazz music, smile and just greet people from all parts of the city. And get you li'l brew on. Drink your li'l beer. Smoke a little Shoshone. But it's mostly about meeting and greeting people.

—Bernard Robertson, Sudan Social and Pleasure Club

While other people may chase big dreams and high-priced items, people from New Orleans, they believe in culture and tradition and family and unity. And I think that's what Mardi Gras Indians bring. It keeps the tradition alive. It keeps the culture alive. And it keeps us united.

—Queen Michelle Hammothe, Queen of the Shining Star Hunters, from *It's Your Glory: The Big Queens of Carnival*

The movements, the music, the attire, the choice of gathering space—all are political expressions. The intricately beaded suits of the Indians and the amazing color combinations the second liners wear can be seen simply as reflecting the aesthetics of the people wearing them. But even in contemporary times, such displays seem to be a reaction to Governor Miró's 1786 decree that black women not pay "excessive attention to dress," that they not wear plumes or jewelry, and that they bind their hair in a kerchief or *tignon*. Of course, Creole women being Creole, they were soon adorning their *tignons* so elaborately that they were looking better than they had any right to look. "Excessive attention to dress" is the hallmark of the black parading tradition. The competition among Mardi Gras Indian gangs is to be the "prettiest," and among mutual aid societies it is to be the most finely outfitted.

The idea that these wild black gyrations and colorful suits somehow constitute an intentional form of political statement is counterintuitive. "Classic theories of political protest envision the body as an agitated irrationality, propelling individuals into the chaos of mob performance," wrote Susan Leigh Foster in her essay "Choreographies of Protest." "Swept up into the fervor of the crowd, the body succumbs to the unpredictable whims of the masses." Foster criticizes such classical theories for their failure to see the body as an "articulate signifying agent." She herself sees the body as "a vast reservoir of signs and symbols . . . capable of both persuasion and obstinate recalcitrance."

Obstinate? Recalcitrant? What better words could there be to describe the African attitude toward the enslavers of New Orleans?

The decision to dance in Congo Square then and on city streets now in ways reminiscent of West Africa is a conscious rebuke to assimilationist black folks and high-society whites who would seek to civilize the black population by whitening it. ("If only they could be more like the Irish . . .") But nothing about second liners and Mardi Gras Indians says "assimilation," and, in a nation so obsessed with homogeneity that its citizens become fearful when they hear other languages being spoken, speaking in this uniquely New Orleanian language of color and rhythm and movement is indeed a political act.

In an era when shootings of unarmed black civilians by officers of the state has spawned a whole movement dedicated to the stating of the obvious (Black Lives Matter), any gathering of black people in public space is political at least insofar as it asserts the right to exercise rights. The history of police violence against black citizens shows that the only thing recent about this official brutality in the service of rights suppression is the fact that it is now captured so often on video.

Rudy Lombard and Jerome Smith, two veterans of the 1960s freedom movement, founded Tambourine & Fan expressly to harness the power of the second line culture in order to make political and economic gains in the black community. They danced and paraded, but they also sought to instill social values in the young people served by the organization. Well aware of the legacy of police brutality against the black community in general and the black parading tradition in particular, Tambourine & Fan once paused its second line through the central business district in front of the old downtown Howard Johnson's hotel to acknowledge Mark Essex. That black gunman shot ten police officers between New Year's Eve 1972 and January 7, 1973, killing three officers from a perch in the hotel after killing two others in an ambush the week before. Perhaps Eduardo Galeano explains it best in his book *Upside Down: A Primer for the Looking Glass World*: "A Chico Buarque song starts out with the wail of a police siren: 'Call the thief! Call the thief!' pleads the Brazilian singer."

Though second line parades and Mardi Gras Indian processions are clear statements on the politics of race, they are also tactical movements in an unrelenting class war. When the Black Men of Labor formed in the 1990s, they made their color and class allegiances clear in the selection of their name. Then they went further, incorporating West African fabrics and patterns in their suits.

Social Aid and Pleasure Clubs put on second line parades throughout the day at the New Orleans Jazz and Heritage Festival. (Photo by Peggy Scott Laborde)

Citing concern over the number of shootings that had taken place around parades, Mayor Ray Nagin and Police Superintendent Warren Riley, both black, raised the parade fees paid by second line organizations by as much as 530 percent. In the case of the Original Pigeon Town Steppers Social Aid and Pleasure Club, that meant an increase from $1,200 in 2005 to $7,560 in 2006. The Mardi Gras parade krewes, which count some of the richest New Orleanians among their members, were paying a mere $750. The Social Aid and Pleasure Club Task Force, with the assistance of the Louisiana ACLU, sued the city in federal court and ultimately got the fees reduced to more sensible increases.

If only the assault on the Indians and second liners were purely fiscal—but the harassment is often physical. There are two sacred days on the Mardi Gras Indian calendar: Mardi Gras and St. Joseph's Day. Any district commander who was ignorant of that was willfully so. On St. Joseph's night in 2005, police with drawn guns and blaring sirens interrupted the traditional gathering. Officers cursed, pushed, harassed, and arrested Indians, offering only rude explanations. Indians present that night have said that if only the officers had expressed their concerns rationally and asked for assistance, things could have been handled without incident.

But perhaps heavily armed New Orleans police officers confronting crowds of dancing, singing, costumed black people understood the political dimension of the spectacle before them. Perhaps they were as fearful of the citizens they were sworn "to protect and to serve" as the South African Defense Force was of their own populace. "Most of the riot police who had to contain those marches were shit-scared of the chanting blacks confronting them," said a former riot police commander, interviewed for the 2002 documentary *Amandla! A Revolution in Four Part Harmony*. "Here was an unarmed mob instilling fear just by their *toyi-toyi*."

The St. Joseph's Night Ambush, as it has come to be called by its victims, culminated in a hearing in the New Orleans City Council chambers convened by Councilman Oliver Thomas. Allison "Tootie" Montana, the legendary big chief of the Yellow Pocahontas Indian gang, spoke. Years before, he had told me that he stopped parading in the French Quarter because of police mistreatment.

Big Chief Tootie Montana collapsed while testifying. Perhaps his heart couldn't take the sudden eruption of renewed outrage and history he was finally able to express at an official gathering. He died in the council chambers.

His last words were, "This has got to stop."

Lolis Eric Elie has written for HBO's Treme *and the documentaries* Faubourg Treme *and* Smokestack Lightning. *A former* Times-Picayune *columnist, he's the author of* Smokestack Lightning: Adventures in the Heart of Barbecue Country *and* Treme: Stories and Recipes From the Heart of New Orleans. *A contributing editor for the* Oxford American, *his essay "America's Greatest Hits" was anthologized in* Best African American Essays of 2010.

The Mercedes-Benz Superdome, formerly known as just the Superdome, has been part of New Orleans since 1975. (Photo by George Long)

Finishing Strong

Marty Mulé

There was Drew Brees quarterbacking the Saints to their "Party with the Lombardi," Michael Jordan hitting a jumper in the last seconds for an NCAA title, Muhammad Ali's last victory—and his third and last championship.

And that's just the tip of the Superdome.

If there is anything that could equal New Orleans' reputation as a culinary paradise or as a musical incubator, it is its role as a sports mecca.

The story of sports in America could hardly be told without a prominent mention of New Orleans. Each of the aforementioned exploits was won not only in New Orleans but also at the very same location—the Mercedes-Benz Superdome. That is one eye-catching fact considering the differences in the three very different sports and the vast differences in each of their required dimensions.

The Superdome has been the linchpin of contemporary sports in the old river town. That mushroomed-shaped protrusion that defines the Crescent City skyline has become a worldwide symbol of high stakes competition.

There have been six college football championship games played there, the last four for the Bowl Championship Series title. A College Football Playoff title game is set for 2020. New Orleans has also hosted five Final Fours and been the site of two memorable boxing events—Muhammad Ali's victory against Leon Spinks in 1978 that made Ali the first three-time heavyweight champion, and Sugar Ray Leonard's "*no mas*" victory against Roberto Duran two years later.

One can say that more champions in more sports have been crowned in the Superdome than any other site anywhere, and that's not to mention it is the home of the NFL's New Orleans Saints and was once the domicile of the NBA's New Orleans Jazz.

Since 1998, the Superdome has had an annex facility—the Smoothie King Center, where the NBA's New Orleans Pelicans now play and two NBA All-Star games and two Women's Final Fours have been contested, among many other sports and entertainment events.

And that's just the big stuff.

Tulane made the Superdome its football home from the building's opening in 1975 until 2014 when the Green Wave moved back to campus to play in 2014. The Bayou Classic between Southern and Grambling has been a staple of Thanksgiving weekend since 1975, and the R+L Carriers New Orleans Bowl has given the city two post-season college football games since 2001.

In the early years of the Dome, there were regular-season college basketball games featuring Tulane, UNO, and other local schools; college baseball showcase events that drew record crowds; Major League Baseball exhibitions, and, for one season, Minor League Baseball, the short-lived revival of the Pelicans. The local Minor League team, formerly the Zephyrs and now the Baby Cakes, has its own stadium in Metairie adjacent to the Saints and Pelicans practice facilities. No facility on the globe has a résumé like the Superdome's. But it's only fitting giving the city's sporting past.

New Orleans is the home of America's oldest tennis club (New Orleans Lawn Tennis Club, founded in 1876), America's second-oldest yacht club (Southern Yacht Club, founded in 1849), and America's third-oldest race track (Fair Grounds, founded in 1872).

New Orleans, among other things, was where fencing was introduced in America and where boxing gloves were first used in a heavyweight championship fight—the 1892 John L. Sullivan-Gentleman Jim Corbett fight. The city also was the site of the longest fight in boxing history (111 rounds between Andy Bowen and Jack Burke in 1893, ending in a "no-contest" after seven hours and nineteen minutes) and the shortest of a featured heavyweight bout (fourteen seconds, in 1918 when Jack Dempsey knocked out Carl Morris); where Lexington and Lecomte ran their series of world-record match races in 1854; where Black Gold, a turf immortal, ran his first and last races and Earl Sande, the master jockey, rode his first winner; where Clara Baer of Newcomb College wrote the first set of rules for girls' basketball in 1895; where baseball's Ladies Day, rain check, and tarpaulins originated; where the 1992 Olympic Track and Field Trials were held.

New Orleans produced Paul Morphy (1837-1884), one of the greatest of all chess masters, and it is where Bernard de Marigny (1785-1868) introduced the dice game craps into this country. It is also the home of the Sugar Bowl, the second oldest of the college post-season games (after the Rose Bowl). Its annual matchup (thanks to historic links with the powerful Southeastern Conference, or SEC) has included the season's national champion team twenty-three times, more than any other bowl game.

The most important New Orleanians of the twentieth century may have been Louis "Satchmo" Armstrong and Dave Dixon—Armstrong as the foremost ambassador of jazz to the world and Dixon because he transformed New Orleans' landscape . . . and turned on a spigot for major-league sports events. New Orleans wouldn't be viewed the same without either one.

Dixon was a local businessman, Tulane alumnus, World War II Marine, and a serious stargazer. He conceived the Superdome concept, which became the force behind New Orleans' status as a modern-day sports destination—indeed, even the reason for an NFL franchise being planted here. None of this would have happened without his vision and boundless energy. The idea of a multipurpose stadium came into his head in the early 1950s when he read of internationally renowned architect Buckminster Fuller being commissioned to design a domed stadium for the Brooklyn Dodgers. That never came to fruition, of course, but Dixon never forgot the idea.

The notion of a New Orleans pro-football team came a few years later when Mayor Chep Morrison was talking about building an updated baseball park on Lake Pontchartrain to

Born Jean-Bernard Xavier Philippe de Marigny de Mandeville, Bernard de Marigny was a prominent and colorful New Orleans French Creole, planter, playboy, politician, gambler, and entrepreneur who developed the city's Faubourg Marigny and the City of Mandeville in St. Tammany Parish. He introduced the city to a dice game that later would become known as craps. Marigny eventually squandered his fortune and died in poverty. (Photograph by A. Constant, circa 1866. Courtesy of The Historic New Orleans Collection.)

save the New Orleans Pelicans Minor League Baseball team (1887-1959), a longtime member of the Southern League, and perhaps at the same time attract Major League Baseball.

Dixon met with the mayor and told him it was football that was the ascending sport and that's what they should pursue. Morrison liked the idea and gave Dixon his blessing to see what could be done—no easy task.

Dixon's quixotic dual missions took years of building contacts, promoting exhibition games, and making incremental inroads, but it got liftoff in 1964 when he found an ally in new Louisiana governor John J. McKeithen, who listened to a presentation by Dixon and then thundered: "*That . . .* would be the greatest building in the history of man! By God, we'll build it."

The original idea when it went before state voters in 1966 was a stadium of 50,000 to 60,000 seats, tailored mainly for football, at a cost of $50 million. The concept grew as Dixon thought of more ways it could be utilized, every one of which McKeithen concurred with.

This being Louisiana, the idea of a new stadium ignited a political firestorm, and it took almost a decade to overcome the obstacles. When it opened in 1975, the Dome, perhaps the most versatile building in the world, had a football seating of 76,000 seats and cost $163 million.

Remember, this was a sum almost fifteen times more than the original Louisiana Purchase. The $11.3 million America paid to Napoleon Bonaparte wouldn't have bought the thirteen acres on which the Superdome now sits.

But the Dome has been worth every penny, long since having paid for itself many times over just in taxes visitors to New Orleans added to the state's coffers in attending premium sports and entertainment events.

With a major assist from the Sugar Bowl, which expanded Tulane Stadium fourfold to 80,000 seats over the decades and gave pro football an immediate and suitable place to play, the Superdome was the hook to lure the Saints here,

Pelican Stadium (1915-1957) was the home of the Triple A New Orleans Pelicans baseball team. It was located on the corner of Tulane Avenue and South Carrollton Avenue, today the site of a storage facility. (Courtesy of The Historic New Orleans Collection)

Gov. John J. McKeithen (1918-1999). The two-term Louisiana governor and Democrat strongly supported construction of the Louisiana Superdome in New Orleans. (Portrait by Harold Edwards Carney, March 1966. Courtesy of The Historic New Orleans Collection.)

John Mecom was the original owner of the New Orleans Saints. He is shown here with Tom Fears, the team's first coach. The team was founded in 1966. (Courtesy of The Historic New Orleans Collection)

An early Saints game at Tulane Stadium. Shown is a scene from an elaborate halftime show. (Courtesy of The Historic New Orleans Collection)

though the team arrived in 1967, eight years before the completion of the Dome. Until then, Tulane Stadium was their home.

Dixon acknowledged the pioneering efforts, both in showing what a sports magnet New Orleans could be and in providing a home for the Saints until the Superdome was ready for occupancy. "We owe a great debt of gratitude to the Sugar Bowl," Dixon said.

It took four years, from groundbreaking to opening, to complete, with 800 construction workers swarming over the project site on a given day. The scope of the Superdome was so vast that it brought forth such stupefying measurements as its 125 million cubic feet of space, the largest unobstructed room ever built by man.

It's a malleable building and has served its purpose with a parade of wide-varying events—from the nomination of a president (George H. W. Bush in 1988) to a papal visit (Pope John Paul II in 1987) to performances by entertainment giants such as Frank Sinatra and the Rolling Stones and even to tractor-trailer pulls. But its real *raison d'être* is housing major-league sports, international and local—just as Dave Dixon envisioned.

For the local populace, the peak of New Orleans' sports history came on February 7, 2010, in Miami, almost a thousand miles away from the Superdome, where the Saints earned the right to be in South Beach by beating the Minnesota Vikings in the NFC Championship game two weeks earlier.

Super Bowl XLIV between the Saints and the Indianapolis Colts was a local get-together of sorts.

In a game highlighted by a gutsy onside kick by New Orleans to open the second half, the favored Colts were moving into position to tie the Saints late in the fourth quarter. Quarterback Peyton Manning, New Orleans native and the scion of early Saints hero Archie Manning, threw toward teammate Reggie Wayne of Marrero. The Saints' Tracy Porter of nearby Port Allen "jumped" the pass, intercepted, and

Dave Dixon in Tulane Stadium, circa 1967. Dixon (1923-2010) was a New Orleans businessman and the prime mover behind the formation of the New Orleans Saints and the building of the Louisiana Superdome. (Photograph by James V. Elmore, courtesy of The Historic New Orleans Collection.)

returned it seventy-four yards for the touchdown that sealed the 31-17 victory.

Not only had a New Orleans team won a world championship, but it also ended more than four decades of futility. It was a catharsis for a region that four years earlier was ground zero for Hurricane Katrina, the most calamitous natural disaster ever to strike the United States.

With the victory, the Saints overcame their sullied past in which the team was perceived as a star-crossed franchise. Despite putting a touchdown on the board in the first fifteen seconds of its history, this was one woebegotten pro-football operation, mismanaged in the front office and misplayed on the field for decades. The Saints didn't have their first winning season for twenty-one years, didn't make the playoffs for twenty-five years, and didn't win their first playoff game for thirty-three years. In the team's first fifteen drafts, they passed on thirty-three future Hall of Fame players.

This team weren't saints as much as martyrs.

That changed drastically when Sean Payton was hired as coach in 2006, and he relentlessly pursued free-agent quarterback Drew Brees. Together, they comprehensively altered the trajectory of the team.

Brees was the fuse for everything that happened in the 16-3 title season of 2009, steering the Saints to the season's 510 points, the most in the NFL, and completing 363 of his 514 passes, a then-NFL record of 70.6 percentage, for 4,620 yards and 34 touchdowns. It all culminated in the Super Bowl victory.

New Orleans Saints quarterback Drew Brees reigned as Bacchus during the Mardi Gras krewe's 2010 parade. (Photo by Judi Bottoni)

Parades and near-constant celebration followed, collectively called "the Party with the Lombardi," the championship trophy named for the legendary Green Bay Packers coach. That all had a special significance for Vince Lombardi's grandson, Joe Lombardi, then the quarterbacks coach of the Saints.

§

"At the time," Michael Jordan said, "it was the biggest moment of my life." Coming from whom it did, this was a mouthful.

Jordan was recalling his first splash on a big stage, and this was the biggest stage on which college basketball had ever been played—the first Final Four in the Superdome on March 29, 1982.

In a glimpse of future Hall of Fame gatherings, North Carolina coach Dean Smith sent out Jordan and James Worthy with their teammates against Georgetown's Patrick Ewing and his fellow Georgetown Hoyas, coached by John Thompson. There were 61,612 spectators in the Dome, the first live mega-crowd to witness the NCAA's "One Shining Moment."

And, in a Final Four crowning that others could be measured by, Jordan gave them a finish for the ages: the Tar Heel freshman hit a sixteen-foot jumper with fifteen seconds to play, after which Worthy received an errant pass to give UNC a 63-62 victory—the first national championship of Smith's celebrated career.

§

When his arms went up, the roar from the 63,000-plus spectators was deafening. The self-proclaimed "Greatest" had just beaten Leon Spinks in a unanimous fifteen-round decision to regain his heavyweight championship—for an unprecedented third time.

Who could have known it would be the last time Muhammad Ali, one of the most popular and charismatic athletes of all time, would ever again thrust his gloves over his head in victory.

The evening of September 15, 1978, in the Superdome was going to be remembered in any case. The redoubtable Ali headlined a Carnival of Champions which drew an indoor record for a crowd that not only filled the seats but also paid more than $7 million—then the biggest gate in boxing history.

New Orleans, as it has done so often in the last 300 years, had once again found its way into sports record books.

Saints flag flies outside the Cabildo on Jackson Square. (Photo by George Long)

Marshall "Marty" Mulé was a sports writer for the New Orleans Times-Picayune *from 1974 to 2005. He was named Louisiana Sports Writer of the Year fourteen times by the National Sportswriters and Broadcasters Association. Mulé also wrote eight books on Louisiana sports. In 2005, he received the Distinguished Service in Journalism Award from the Louisiana Sports Writers Association. Mulé was active with the Louisiana Sports Hall of Fame, which published a compilation of his sports articles. Marty Mulé died March 12, 2016. His obituary included this quote from newspaper executive Mark Lorando: "There have been many great sports writers in the long history of the* Times-Picayune, *but there has never been a more gifted storyteller than Marty Mulé. His unfailing good humor and kind, collegial manner were gifts to all who worked with him."*

Assistance provided by Ted Lewis.

Gathering the Blocks

Sally Asher

New Orleans has many monikers—the Big Easy, the Crescent City, the Big N.O., the City that Care Forgot, the Pleasure City—all recognizing its multifaceted identities. Nicknames are usually bestowed (wanted or not) from affection or derision, and sometimes there is direct discord between perception and presentation. In 1919, New Orleans spent $100,000 on a national advertising campaign to supplant the city's best-known nickname (the City that Care Forgot) with "New Orleans, City of New Opportunity." In an attempt to rebrand itself, the city focused on the enterprise of its maritime port instead of the availability of its ambrosial ports (as well other wines, whiskeys, and cocktails). Obviously, the less-catchy campaign failed, and a hundred years later, New Orleans is still referred to as the City that Care Forgot. But New Orleans is equally famous for its street names, and these, unlike nicknames, are chosen—not given—and represent the city's desire to define its own identity.

As far back as antebellum times, newspapers wrote about the city's unusual street names. New Orleanians took pride that they named their streets after individuals, events, and ideas that expressed their character from its foundation to its present. "What would West Forty-fifth or East Twenty-seventh Street mean to us?" the *Times-Picayune* wrote in 1904. Citizens recognized even then that streets are more than thoroughfares or geographical markers; they are cultural identifiers that often serve to memorialize or signify what a society deems historically significant. When a city's collective memory is inscribed into geography, it evokes numerous and often conflicting interpretations of its past and its vision of the future. New Orleans, which has been admired (and admonished) for its creative pathways to the past, has had a difficult transition into the modern era of public commemoration, especially with regard to women and African Americans. The chronology of New Orleans' street names is rooted in royalty steeped in hedonistic birthright, saints swathed in righteous reverence, and plantation owners planted in privilege.

In 1721, Canadian explorer Jean-Baptiste Le Moyne, Sieur de Bienville, sent a secret copy of engineer Adrien de Pauger's map of New Orleans to Paris for consideration to be named the capital of French Louisiana. The map served multiple purposes. It demonstrated the city's strategic location on high ground along a bend of the Mississippi and was a tool of adulation. The city itself, *La Nouvelle-Orléans,* was named after the then-regent of France, Philip II, Duke of Orleans, a man whom the French philosopher Voltaire described as a "man of few scruples." His various affairs, rumors of murder, and whispers of an incestuous relationship with his daughter no doubt inspired this depiction. But the duke wasn't the only one honored. New Orleans' first street names were an elegant grid of flattery to the royal family and a sign of its devotion to Catholicism. Of the original fourteen streets, eight were named for royalty (including four of Louis XIV's illegitimate children) and four were named after Catholic saints. And be it geography, luck, ego, or impatience, New Orleans was named the new colonial capital. Its culture of naming streets would continue in an exceptional parade of vice and virtue, privilege and privation.

As New Orleans grew beyond the French Quarter, more private plantations were sliced into public faubourgs (suburbs). One of the privileges of subdividing one's plantation was naming the streets within it. Many chose the familial route, giving streets their surnames or the names of beloved ones: Amelia, Arabella, Clouet, Delachaise, Dufossat, Hurst, Leontine, Octavia, Poeyfarre, Soniat, Toledano, Treme. Others honored popular religious, political, and military leaders. At one point, there were more than half a dozen John the Baptist, Napoleon, and Washington Streets. In the 1860s, an ordinance was passed to limit streets to one name—two at the most, but only if one was above Canal Street (where the Americans predominantly resided) and one below it (where the Creoles primarily lived). After the French Revolution, the classics came into vogue and likely influenced surveyor Barthelemy Lafon in naming nine adjacent streets after the nine muses—Calliope, Clio, Erato, Euterpe, Melpomene, Polymnia, Terpsichore, Thalia, Urania—and their nearby kin—Dryades and Euphrosine. While plantation owners and city surveyors had considerable influence on New Orleans' street names, one man had more influence over the nomenclature than any other in the city's history.

Bernard de Marigny was a wealthy Creole born in 1785. His father died when he was a teenager, and the young Marigny inherited a considerable estate. He navigated his wealth with elegance, intelligence, civic-mindedness, and a dose of debauchery. He also named some of his streets after family and military leaders, but unlike others who named streets only after individuals, Marigny named many after his passions: Craps (after the game he is credited with bringing to the United States and the rumored cause of the loss of some of his fortune; after protests from some churches, it was changed to the more respectable Burgundy), Genius (now Galvez), Good Children (now St. Claude), Liberals (now Miro), Love (now North Rampart), and Peace (now Kerlerec). Many of his original street names still remain: Abundance, Agriculture, Arts, Duels, Elysian Fields, Hope, Industry, Law, Music, Painters, Treasure, and, most famously, Frenchmen.

The era of individuals naming streets ended around the Civil War and gave way to a new era of codification and civic consideration. In 1852, 1894, and 1924, the city made sweeping street name changes, eliminating or altering hundreds under new ordinances. Since then, street name changes have been less expansive and primarily done on a case-by-case basis and under the consideration of public opinion.

In the early twentieth century, women started

Desire Street is among the many of New Orleans streets still demarcated by the old-style blue and white tiles in the sidewalk. (Photo by Sally Asher)

showing up in the city's landscape for their deeds, not for their familial standing. Margaret Place was named after Margaret "Mother of Orphans" Haughery. The illiterate, penniless, widowed Irish immigrant worked as a laundress and eventually invested in a local bakery, turning it into the largest bakery in the United States. She died in 1882, was given a state funeral, and left more than $30,000 to the city's orphans. But the street named after her is a scant one block long. Similar is Sophie Wright Place. Wright, a crippled woman born in 1866, opened the Home Institute for Girls, started the city's first free night school, and was essential in establishing a summer sanctuary in St. Tammany Parish for working women and their children. She was dubbed the "South's Most Useful Citizen," and twelve years after her death in 1912, a two-block street in the Lower Garden District was named after her. Over time, however, the length of streets named after women grew. In 1989, New Orleans honored Oretha Castle Haley, a black civil rights activist and community leader, with a boulevard approximately eleven blocks long. In 2012, Henriette Delille, a free woman of color born in 1813 who cofounded the Sisters of the Holy Family, a black congregation that exists to this day, had an eight-block street in Treme named for her. Currently, Delille is "venerable," two steps removed from being recognized as a saint. Honoring women with street names in New Orleans is still somewhat novel but far less controversial than naming streets after black men.

In 1977, New Orleans honored Martin Luther King Jr. with a street, changing a thirty-five-block stretch of Melpomene (the muse of tragedy) to Martin Luther King Jr. Boulevard. Some believed that the naming was trivialized because it was in a predominantly black neighborhood and essentially ended at a white neighborhood. Many argued that renaming Canal Street would have been a more appropriate honor. Disagreements raged again in 1989 when a proposal was introduced to change the remaining section of Melpomene after King. Sharp criticism came from various historical and preservationist organizations.

This brightly colored mural on the backside of the Young Leadership Council faces Oretha Castle Haley Boulevard and is emblematic of the street's vibrant comeback. (Photograph by Sally Asher)

Henriette Delille, cofounder of the Sisters of the Holy Family and the first native-born African American whose pathway to sainthood has been officially established by the Catholic Church, has a street named after her and an inconspicuous plaque on the sidewalk behind St. Louis Cathedral. (Photograph by Sally Asher)

Eventually, a compromise was struck: Martin Luther King Jr. Boulevard halted at St. Charles Avenue—a metaphorical and physical divide between black and white neighborhoods. In contrast, the following year, cartoonist and historian John Churchill Chase—who protested the changing of the 200-year-old Front Street to Convention Center Boulevard in 1983, calling it "historical heresy"—was honored with a street name four years after his death. Part of Calliope (the muse of poetry) was renamed. It is perhaps fitting that the goddess of tragedy was associated with a martyr for civil rights and that the goddess of poetry was associated with a writer.

Local civil rights activist A. P. Tureaud faced similar challenges. Tureaud was born in 1899 and got his law degree in 1925, becoming one of the few African American lawyers in Louisiana at that time. He worked with the NAACP, helping to desegregate most of the New Orleans' public schools before the Civil Rights Act of 1964. Less than ten years after his death in 1972, a movement started to rename part of London Avenue after Tureaud. Complaints arose that it sounded too much like Touro Street and that citizens were left out of the process. City Council meetings dissolved into name-calling matches between citizens and officials, and Mayor Ernest "Dutch" Morial said he hadn't foreseen the outcry it created, stating there were "deeper reasons for the opposition." Eventually, the city council voted five to one in favor of the change.

More than thirty years later, challenges and questions over naming streets to honor black men persist. In 2015, an ordinance was introduced to change sections of Carondelet Street to Robert C. Blakes Sr. Drive and Lasalle Street to Rev. John Raphael Jr. Way. Raphael was a former New Orleans police officer who became a pastor at the New Hope Baptist Church. He did missionary work overseas and led crusades to stop violence by posting Thou Shalt Not Kill signs. Blakes founded New Hope Ministries, worked to reduce blight and crime, and ran a weekly outreach to feed the homeless. Both men died in 2013. The proposed ordinance not only ignited accusations of political pandering but also violated various criteria for street name changes. For current consideration, an honoree needs to be deceased for no fewer than five years; the renaming cannot fragment any continuous street (the entire street needs to be renamed, or the section of the street needs to be physically separated from other portions of the street); and no titles (Honorable, King, Dr., etc.) or punctuation (including periods, dashes, commas, etc.) are allowed. The proposed renaming in 2015 violated all of these. The City Council meetings were volatile, council members traded vitriolic barbs, and citizens spoke out passionately for or against the changes. A compromise was suggested to give the men honorary street names (which are typically designated by the color brown instead of blue) and require no official changing of residential and business addresses. Those in favor of the name change claimed the compromise was an insult to the men's contributions. In the end, the streets were renamed. Some viewed it as a victory for the commemoration of men whose devotion bettered their city and community, but others worried about the precedent it set with regard to proper procedure and protocol. The aftereffects of these renamings are, as yet, unclear.

Memory, geography, and history all course through New Orleans' streets. Over time, views on historical significance and memorialization have evolved, and these changing views and values are manifested in the urban landscape. These public battles present a distilled picture of the motivations and values of citizens and the challenges the city faces. Perhaps poetically emblematic of the challenges and emotions, in 2002, a street was named after cornetist Buddy Bolden. The musician, who is believed to be the first bandleader to play jazz,

IN MEMORY OF
CHARLES JOSEPH "BUDDY" BOLDEN
SEPTEMBER 6, 1877 — NOVEMBER 4, 1931

IN AN UNMARKED GRAVE NEAR HERE RESTS
BUDDY BOLDEN
LEGENDARY CORNET PLAYER
NEW ORLEANS JAZZ PIONEER
AND FIRST "KING OF JAZZ"

"THE BLOWINGEST MAN SINCE GABRIEL"
--JELLY ROLL MORTON

"King of the Cornet" Buddy Bolden has a one-block street named after him leading to Holt Cemetery, where he lies in an unmarked grave and is honored by a recently built monument. (Photograph by Sally Asher)

was honored with a little-known one-block street. The *Times-Picayune* wrote that it was sad enough that Bolden died in obscurity and was buried in an unmarked grave without also giving him an "obscure memorial." (He is buried at Holt Cemetery, near Delgado College.) Years later, a fan had a tombstone made. Ralph Waldo Emerson famously wrote, "Life is a journey, not a destination," but for many in New Orleans, neither the journey nor the destination is as important as the name of the street they are traveling on to get there.

Sally Asher is the author of Hope & New Orleans: A History of Crescent City Street Names *and* Stories from the St. Louis Cemeteries of New Orleans. *She holds two master's degrees from Tulane University and has been the public relations photographer since 2008. She frequently lectures on New Orleans history through the Louisiana State Museum. Most recently, Asher has worked on a book about Prohibition in New Orleans for LSU Press.*

Ursuline nuns arrived in New Orleans from France on August, 7, 1727. Among the facilities they operated is a school for girls, which continues to this day. (Courtesy of The Historic New Orleans Collection)

Creating a New Culture

Patricia Brady

New Orleans was always a multiracial society: Women helped create a new culture and a new people. Its first women were Chitimacha and Acolapissa Indians. Some married or lived with the tough Frenchmen who cleared the cypresses and built the city; others were enslaved, purchased as servants or concubines. Yet they aren't remembered as the city's foremothers; not even their names are recorded. At the city's market, they remained a presence through the nineteenth century, selling herbal remedies, baskets, and filé, the ground sassafras leaves used in filé gumbo. They disappeared gradually as both tribes withdrew into southwestern Louisiana. But their genetic traces still linger among New Orleans Creoles.

Contributing to the city's mélange, the first of many slave ships arrived in Louisiana in 1719. These 450 Africans were largely ethnic Bambaras purchased in Juda (now Ouidah, Benin), West Africa. The ships' captains were instructed to select slaves who were experienced rice farmers and to buy barrels of rice for seeding. Women in Africa farmed alongside men, so together they introduced rice cultivation—as well as okra, melons, and corn—to Louisiana. They also brought with them Voudou, their music, dance, cookery, folk tales, and other aspects of their culture.

In the half-century that France held Louisiana, authorities tried to impose a social order based on Catholic marriage between whites. Unfortunately for their plans, very few French women would come to New Orleans, other than wives of colonial officers and administrators. The imbalance between poorer white men and women often ran as high as five to one. To remedy this deficit, authorities exported women prisoners, prostitutes, and orphaned girls from France to the colony. Nonetheless, interracial couplings among blacks, whites, Native Americans, and every mixture in between continued despite official disapproval.

Catholicism was such an integral part of French culture that civil authorities and priests determined that nuns should run hospitals and schools. Finally, the Ursulines, an order dedicated to the education of young women, arrived in 1727. Besides running a boarding school and day schools, an orphanage, and a hospital, they cared for the elderly and abused wives. Their schools were not for whites only; they also included blacks, Native Americans, and girls of mixed race. Because of them, more women than men were literate for years to come.

Shortly after the introduction of Africans to Louisiana, individual slaves were freed. Manumission continued during the French period, but the number of free people of color grew rapidly after Spanish control was established in 1769.

The Haitian Revolution of 1791 also had profound effects in Louisiana. Thousands of whites and free people of color, along with their slaves, fled the island then known as Saint-Domingue. After the Louisiana Purchase, the American governor allowed about 10,000 of those refugees to enter the territory in 1809 and 1810. Their presence reinforced French language and culture, Catholicism, and Voudou and nearly doubled the number of free people of color in New Orleans.

After Louisiana became a state in 1812, English-speaking white Protestant men flocked to New Orleans. Many of them published their observations of a city that was exotic and foreign to them. The status of free people of color—their great number, sophistication, stylishness, and open association with whites—was a revelation. Free women of color were everywhere. They were the most faithful attendants at Mass in St. Louis Cathedral, vendors at the market and in the streets, shop owners, dressmakers, hairdressers, boarding house keepers, herbalists, and sometime-companions of white men. The perceived vision of these women has been skewed, however, by the prejudices and misinformation of the men who wrote about them.

The legendary quadroon balls, attended by women of color and white men only, began during the early nineteenth century but were never central to Creole society. By the 1830s they were essentially prurient tourist events, visited by white men who came to the city to be shocked, titillated, or disgusted after they had gazed their fill. Most free women of color preferred to marry men from their own community with established economic and social positions. In the early days, the imbalance in their numbers made that choice possible for only a few. Because interracial marriage was illegal, free women of color became the unmarried sexual companions of white men, sometimes briefly, many for a lifetime. Despite increasing legal difficulties, men in long-term relationships usually left their estates to their companions and children. Their descendants are still visible and prominent in all aspects of public life in New Orleans.

Women enjoyed the right to maintain and control separate estates as a result of laws introduced during Spanish colonial rule. Unlike women in the British colonies, they could protect inheritances, investments, or earnings from avaricious or unwise husbands. One woman grateful for this provision was Micaela Almonester (1795-1874), who became the Baroness de Pontalba through an arranged marriage. After moving to France, her life became a painful melodrama as her father-in-law made every effort, including attempted murder, to gain control of her money. Returning to New Orleans in the 1840s, she regained control of her estate through local courts. While here, she built facing rows of elegant red-brick town houses on inherited property along both sides of Jackson Square.

Many other women helped make New Orleans what it is today. Marie Laveau (1801-1881), a free woman of color, is one of the city's most famous characters. She was a devout Catholic who lived modestly and tended the sick and needy and was a famed practitioner of Voudou. Newspapers sensationalized her

Mother Frances Xavier Cabrini, America's first saint, founded an orphanage in New Orleans in 1892. She became the United States' first saint, since she became a naturalized citizen. She ultimately founded sixty-seven institutions, including schools and hospitals. The orphanage is now a girls' high school. (From the collection of Peggy Scott Laborde)

Micaela Almonester, Baroness Pontalba, built these apartments flanking Jackson Square in 1849. (Courtesy of The Historic New Orleans Collection)

ceremonies, which white women attended, as scandalous orgies. Her tomb in St. Louis Cemetery I is vandalized repeatedly by people fantasizing about Voudou and vampires.

Another free woman of color, Henriette Delille (1812-1862), was unable to join the Ursulines because of her race. With a few like-minded friends, she committed herself to a lifetime of service to the sick, the poor, and the uneducated among free people and slaves. In 1842, the women were recognized as the Sisters of the Holy Family. They have had a profound effect on the lives of black Catholics in New Orleans. They founded a nursing home, orphanage, and St. Mary's Academy, which has educated generations of girls. The Vatican opened the canonization process for Mother Henriette Delille in 1988. Soon New Orleans should have its first native-born saint and one of the world's few black saints.

During the nineteenth century, thousands of immigrants fled famine and repression in Ireland. Margaret Gaffney Haughery (1813-1882) arrived here in 1835, bereft of family or friends, penniless, and uneducated. A city plagued by yellow fever, dysentery, and other diseases teemed with orphans. An orphan herself, she dedicated her life to them. To feed the needy children, Haughery started a dairy and a bakery. Finding an unexpected talent for business, she became the city's richest and most successful woman; her immense fortune was left to orphanages and other charities in New Orleans. Revered as "Mother of Orphans" and "Saint Margaret," her memory survives today with a statue on Prytania Street, inscribed simply "Margaret."

The redoubtable Eliza Jane Nicholson (1843-1896) was a tiny snub-nosed redhead from Mississippi, a poet who called herself Pearl Rivers. In 1876 she inherited the *Picayune*, a floundering newspaper deep in debt. She became the first woman publisher in the South, the second in the nation. Nicholson edited every word herself, introduced new features, and promoted such women writers as Dorothy Dix at equal pay with men. Under her leadership, the *Picayune* became one of the nation's leading papers.

In 1960, desegregation of a previously all-white public school, the first in the South, fell on one little girl. Ruby Bridges was six when she entered William Frantz Elementary School. Escorted by federal marshals, she ran a gauntlet of screaming white women who cursed and threatened to kill her. She spent the entire year taught by one teacher and ostracized by other students. The next year things improved, and she was able to finish her education and enjoy a successful career and family life out of the glare of publicity. In the 1990s Bridges established a foundation to encourage tolerance and today occasionally talks publicly about her ordeal.

Oretha Castle (1939-1987) was only twenty when she joined picket lines on Dryades Street demanding decent jobs for blacks in the stores where they shopped. She cofounded a chapter of CORE (Congress of Racial Equality) and defeated a man to become its president. Sit-ins, protests, marches, voter registration drives, and politics were her tools; she later forced the integration of the city's public parks. As an administrator at Charity Hospital, she focused attention on sickle cell anemia and other black health issues. Two years after her death, the city renamed a portion of Dryades Street in her honor. Oretha Castle Haley Boulevard is today a symbol of urban revitalization.

Lindy Claiborne Boggs (1916-2013) got her start in politics as the wife of Hale Boggs, a Democrat who represented New Orleans in the US House of Representatives for twenty-six years. As a strategist and eloquent speaker, she was with him all the way. After his death in 1973, she was elected to serve out his term, the first woman from Louisiana elected to national office. Boggs was

The illiterate Irishwoman Margaret Gaffney Haughery became a successful entrepreneur and philanthropist who built a fortune that she dedicated to the care of orphans and other charities. (Brooch, circa 1885. Courtesy of The Historic New Orleans Collection)

Eliza Jane Nicholson was a journalist, poet, literary editor, a champion for women writers, and first woman publisher of a major daily Louisiana newspaper, the New Orleans Daily Picayune. *Writing under the name of Pearl Rivers, Nicholson inherited the* Picayune *from her first husband, Alva Holbrook. In 1878, she married George Nicholson. (Photograph by Eugene Simon, circa 1892. Courtesy of The Historic New Orleans Collection)*

reelected eight more times before her retirement in 1991. For the last seven years, she was the only white representative in the nation from a majority-black district. Always supportive of women's issues, Boggs notably fought for equal credit access. Her daughter, Cokie Roberts, though born in New Orleans, has made her career in Washington, first as a reporter and political commentator, then as a best-selling author and speaker on women's issues and history.

American life has been enriched by other New Orleanians—Donna Brazile, Kitty Carlisle, Patricia Clarkson, Ellen DeGeneres, Lillian Hellman, Dorothy Lamour, Adah Isaacs Mencken, and Madam C. J. Walker, to name a few. One of the most famous of these émigrés is Mahalia Jackson (1911-1972). Growing up poor, she found joy singing at the family's Baptist church. At sixteen, she headed to Chicago, where she lived for the rest of her life. Her gospel performances and records made her internationally famous and wealthy. From the 1950s on, she sang at civil rights fundraisers and rallies, including the March on Washington in 1963. The Theatre for the Performing Arts in New Orleans was renamed in her honor in 1993.

In a city where queens of Carnival krewes rule, popular culture also has its royalty. We have Mahalia Jackson, "Queen of Gospel"; Irma Thomas, "Soul Queen of New Orleans"; and Leah Chase and Ella Brennan, "Queens of Creole Cuisine." "It's Raining" could be our civic anthem, given our weather. Like Jackson, Irma Thomas grew up singing in a Baptist church but went on to international success in soul, blues, and R&B. But for all her fame, New Orleans loves her best. She appears annually at the Jazz and Heritage Festival and headlines the Mother's Day celebration at Audubon Zoo. Now in her seventies, she still belts out her hits and brings audiences to their feet.

Music and food run neck-and-neck as love objects in New Orleans. In most cities, men dominate the restaurant world; here, two longtime stars are Leah Chase of Dooky Chase's and Ella Brennan of Commander's Palace. Between

Patricia Clarkson was nominated for the Academy Award for Best Supporting Actress and the Golden Globe for her performance in Pieces of April *(2003). She twice won the Primetime Emmy Award for Outstanding Guest Actress in a Drama Series for her recurring role in* Six Feet Under. *In 2015, she was nominated for a Tony Award for her performance in* The Elephant Man. *Clarkson has provided narration for many series by Ken Burns.* (Photo by Joella Marano)

New Orleans-born gospel singer Mahalia Jackson and Duke Ellington at the First New Orleans Jazz and Heritage Festival, 1970. George Wein, jazz fest producer, is seen standing near a man with a video camera. Pleasant Joseph, "Cousin Joe" (1907-1989), stands at the right. (Photograph by Michael P. Smith, 1970. Courtesy of The Historic New Orleans Collection.)

Born Mary Leta Dorothy Slaton in New Orleans, Dorothy Lamour (1914-1996) was a popular screen actress and singer best known as the "Sarong Queen" for her roles in movies such as Paramount's six Road films with Bob Hope and Bing Crosby. (Courtesy of The Historic New Orleans Collection)

them, they've won every food award in the business and maintained a devoted following. Leah Chase learned to cook Creole style from her mother. After she and her husband took over Dooky Chase's in the 1940s, it became *the* black restaurant for an elegant night out. Her cooking, stylish décor, and display of works by notable African American artists ensured its success. Public spaces and events in New Orleans were segregated until late 1965; Chase provided private rooms in the early 1960s for civil rights leaders to hold strategy meetings with white supporters without fearing arrest. The restaurant is still on the must-go list of visiting celebrities, including two presidents of the United States.

Ella Brennan began working at her brother's French Quarter restaurant when she was a teenager. She helped open Brennan's on Royal Street in 1946 and took over Commander's Palace uptown in 1974. Never a cook, she excelled in restaurant management, finding and nurturing a series of now-famous chefs. She combined impeccable service and "Haute Creole," an adventurous take on local cookery. Expanding the Brennan empire, she mentored her children, nieces, and nephews. Today, some of the city's top restaurants belong to this extended family. A second generation of accomplished women now runs Commander's—her daughter, Ti Martin, and niece Lally Brennan.

When Hurricane Katrina hit New Orleans, thousands of residents stayed to ride it out. After the storm passed on August 29, 2005, the damage by wind and rain was manageable. Then the water came. Faulty federal levees along drainage and navigation canals broke during the storm surge, flooding 80 percent of the city. Congress initially blamed New Orleanians for living in the wrong place and refused to allocate relief funds. Mary Landrieu, then-US senator and member of a local political dynasty, swung into action to change this perception. She was assisted when Anne Milling, a prominent civic leader, formed Women of the Storm, which included a diverse group of local women from all walks of life. They effectively pressured members of Congress to see for themselves the city's desperate need and vote for federal assistance.

For all the individual achievements touched on here, thousands more women have contributed to the city's culture over the past three centuries. Like Paris, her colonial mother city, New Orleans has been portrayed as a woman in the romantic sense—charming, changeable, alluring, and often dangerous. All true, but New Orleans is better represented by her actual women—determined and strong enough to face any challenge.

Patricia Brady is a social and cultural historian. She has a PhD in history from Tulane University and served as director of publications at The Historic New Orleans Collection for twenty years. She has written extensively about Martha Washington and her family; among her works are Nelly Custis Lewis's Housekeeping Book, George Washington's Beautiful Belly, *and* Martha Washington: An American Life. *Brady is also the author of* A Being So Gentle: The Frontier Love Story of Rachel and Andrew Jackson.

Irma Thomas is one of the city's most beloved music performers. She has been singing since the 1950s. (Courtesy of The Historic New Orleans Collection)

Leah Chase (born January 6, 1923) is a New Orleans chef, author, and television personality. A longtime advocate for African American art and Creole cooking, her restaurant, Dooky Chase, was known as a gathering place during the 1960s among many who participated in the civil rights movement. The interior of her restaurant is filled with art from African American artists. (Photo by Peggy Scott Laborde)

Message from WYES-TV

Allan Pizzato,
President and Chief Executive Officer

We here at WYES have always been about education and being local. That has included conventional television and now digital opportunities as well as print. This book is another way of fulfilling our mission in a lasting way. It is an essential part of WYES' multi-year project, which includes documentaries, a video collection of 200 tricentennial moments, electronic field trips for students, tourism tie-ins, and our special tricentennial website, wyes.org/local/tricentennial.

WYES is proud to be a part of telling our region's continuing story. We look forward to the chapters to follow.

WYES-TV Tricentennial Project
Cornerstone Sponsors

WYES-TV gratefully acknowledges The Historic New Orleans Collection as a Cornerstone Sponsor.

Located in the heart of the French Quarter, The Historic New Orleans Collection is a museum, research center, and publisher dedicated to preserving the history and culture of New Orleans and the surrounding region. THNOC was founded in 1966 by Gen. L. Kemper Williams and Leila Hardie Moore Williams—collectors of Louisiana materials who wished to share their holdings with the public.

Today, THNOC holds over one million items relating to the French Quarter and the colonial era of New Orleans, as well as jazz, literature, decorative arts, photography, and film. THNOC also publishes award-winning original books exploring the history, art, music, culture, and decorative arts of the region. Members of the public are invited to visit THNOC, housed in a cluster of historic buildings in the French Quarter. Visitors may experience the collections through the museum galleries, guided tours, or study in the Williams Research Center.

The exhibits in THNOC's museum galleries depict the multicultural stories of the region, from permanent displays exploring the evolution of Louisiana to rotating exhibitions showcasing local history and fine art. Visitors may explore the galleries on their own at no charge, or join in guided tours that offer exclusive glimpses of the founders' elegant residence and the evolving architectural styles of the city's oldest neighborhood.

The Williams Research Center is free and open to the public, whether dedicated scholars or casual history buffs. With the help of THNOC's experienced reading room staff, visitors can access traditional library items such as books, pamphlets, and periodicals, as well as photographs, prints, drawings, and paintings that illustrate the region's rich history.

More information about THNOC is available online at www.hnoc.org.

WYES-TV gratefully acknowledges the Arlene and Joseph Meraux Charitable Foundation as a Cornerstone Sponsor.

The Meraux Foundation was established by Arlene Meraux to benefit the community of St. Bernard Parish. Guided by her vision, the private family foundation is implementing an innovative strategy to create lasting change. The strategy focuses on four key program areas: educational initiatives, special projects, community building, and land strategies.

The foundation's educational initiatives include annual scholarships to local high school graduates. To date, it has awarded more than 660 scholarships valued at $1.9 million. To further advance educational opportunities, the foundation has granted $1.8 million to develop the Cultural Arts Center of Chalmette High School, sponsors the St. Bernard Performing Arts Academy, and supports scores of educational programs—like the Mississippi River Delta Institute and LSU's AgMagic on the River. Notably, to provide a world-class facility for the students of St. Bernard Parish, the foundation donated land for the new Arlene Meraux Elementary School.

The foundation's special projects include Docville Farm, a 130 acre center dedicated to charity; Studio Arabi, an arts campus to accelerate the cultural economy; Startup St. Bernard, a pitch competition to attract and retain entrepreneurs; Working on the Water, a program to support local fishermen; and the Mississippi River Delta Educational Initiative, an interactive educational program about the Delta's natural and cultural history.

The foundation's community building programs are designed to bring people together and facilitate civil discourse. It hosts and sponsors many events throughout the year, ranging from festivals to informational meetings. The foundation leverages its network and links people and organizations together to address some of St. Bernard Parish's most pressing issues, like coastal protection and economic development.

The foundation's land strategies include leveraging properties to strengthen St. Bernard Parish, such as providing plots for a hospital, sheriff's substation, elementary school, and wetland observation center.

In addition to the customary functions of nonprofits, the Meraux Foundation manages, maintains, and preserves extensive and diverse landholdings. Each type of land poses complex and often delicate challenges in its preservation, protection, and use, but the Meraux Foundation aims to maximize both short- and long-term benefits for the community and ecosystem.

Learn more about the Meraux Foundation at merauxfoundation.org.

Index